I0825526

Praise for

Friends Matter, for Life

"Friendships are the antidote to loneliness. Kimberly Horn's book, *Friends Matter, for Life* is an inspiring book that highlights the healing power of having friends. Her 8 tenets of friendship are thought-provoking and a guiding light on how we can nurture our friendships and grow our inner strength and well-being."

— **Catherine Duncan,** MA, BCC, author of *Everyday Awakening*

"Dr. Horn's compelling arguments over friendship shed light on the cornerstones of a meaningful life. Vital attributes of friendship like empathy illustrate basic human needs well into adulthood. The 8 tenets are a fascinating read and ensure deep meaning for those looking to find understanding and comfort in their connections. Thank you to Dr. Horn for her strong, refreshing, and vital literary contribution."

— **Najma Khorrami,** MPH, author of *A Spoonful of Gratitude*

"Friendships are the cornerstone of life. In her new book, Dr. Kimberly Horn guides us through the dynamic process of evolving relationships and reminds us that being a friend to ourselves is the most important relationship of all."

— **Dana Killion,** author of *Where the Shadows Dance*

"Kimberly Horn's book couldn't come at a better time. We're facing what many are calling a global epidemic of loneliness and isolation. She reminds us that there are different types of friendships, all of which are important for us to nurture and not take for granted. She gives us leave to mourn but also release ourselves from those relationships that have become toxic. And she couches her suggestions within an actionable framework, coupled with forward-looking positive scenarios and introspective, reflective exercises."

— **Eileen Drage O'Reilly,** former president, National Press Club (2023); science writer; Managing Editor of Standards & Training, *Axios*

"One of the most crucial skills you need as an adult is to know how to make new friends; yet nobody teaches you that. Until now. Dr. Kimberly Horn has the science-backed strategies you need for making real, lasting adult friendships."

—**Mel Robbins,** *New York Times* bestselling author and host of *The Mel Robbins Podcast*

"In *Friends Matter, for Life*, Kimberly Horn masterfully addresses how crucial friendships are to health, offering a heartfelt, actionable guide to combating loneliness and nurturing the connections vital to our well-being."

—**Leana Wen,** MD, newspaper columnist, television commentator, and author of *Lifelines: A Doctor's Journey in the Fight for Public Health*

"As much a call to action as a meditation on the importance of the people we choose to spend our lives with, *Friends Matter, for Life* is the antidote to modern feelings of loneliness and distance. Dr. Horn prompts us to think critically and emotionally about ourselves and the relationships we build with others, and in a sincere, authentic way."

—**Charlene Wheeless,** author of *You Are Enough! Reclaiming Your Career and Your Life with Purpose, Passion, and Unapologetic Authenticity*

Friends Matter, for Life

HARNESSING THE 8 TENETS *of* DYNAMIC FRIENDSHIP

friends matter, *for life*

DR. KIMBERLY HORN

amplify
an imprint of Amplify Publishing Group

www.amplifypublishinggroup.com

Friends Matter, for Life: Harnessing the 8 Tenets of Dynamic Friendship

For more information, please contact:
Amplify Publishing, an imprint of Amplify Publishing Group
620 Herndon Parkway, Suite 220
Herndon, VA 20170
info@amplifypublishing.com

Library of Congress Control Number: 2024901244

CPSIA Code: PRV0524A

ISBN-13: 979-8-89138-095-0

Printed in the United States

This book is dedicated to the treasured individuals who have filled my life with love, laughter, support, and meaningful connections. To my beloved "besties," my unforgettable "quad," my cherished "posse," my dear mother and loving spouse, and all of the friends I've encountered on my journey. Whether for a fleeting moment or many years, with ease or complication, each of you has left an indelible mark and imparted the invaluable lessons of dynamic friendship. I am deeply grateful for your presence in my life.

CONTENTS

FOREWORD

Friendship is an ideal conduit for both offering and receiving the love and connection that our world so deeply needs right now.

—Kimberly Horn

Welcome to *Friends Matter, for Life*. This book will take you on a heartfelt journey to understand the profound significance of friendships; it is a guide on how to cultivate and cherish these dynamic connections throughout our lives. As the author, I poured my heart and soul into this book, aiming to provide wisdom and guidance on this beautiful friendship journey.

In a world that sometimes overlooks the power of friendships, this book serves as a reminder of their enduring potential to enrich our lives—at every stage of life. Friends are the family we choose for ourselves, becoming increasingly precious as we age. They are our pillars of support, our sources of joy, and our lifelines in times of need.

This book is unique in its exploration of the complexities of friendships. It acknowledges that people and friendships are intricate and ever-changing—they are dynamic—and despite our desires to have close ties, achieving these connections as adults is not always easy. Within these pages, we will embark on a journey of discovery, uncovering the layers of emotions, challenges, and growth that friendships bring. Drawing on research, personal experiences, and honest anecdotes, the book provides readers with a practical framework for achieving and maintaining dynamic friendships. This book aims to resonate with anyone choosing to walk the path of friendship, providing valuable guidance and support for deepening connections. It will affirm the priceless role of friendships for some of you and introduce new perspectives to others. Ultimately, my hope is that it uplifts you, regardless of where you are on your friendship journey.

In reading *Friends Matter, for Life*, you will come to understand the gifts of embracing the diversity of friendships. Each friend brings a unique perspective, background, and set of experiences to your friendships. Embracing this diversity opens doors to growth, learning, and mutual understanding, making our friendships vibrant and enriching. Authentic communication emerges as a guiding principle, reminding us of the power of open and honest conversations. Adapting to the evolving dynamics of friendships becomes a graceful skill as you navigate the changes that naturally occur over time. Trust and loyalty will take center stage, forming connections that withstand the tests of time.

The importance of investing time and energy into our friendships is a recurring theme. The book encourages you to celebrate your friends' milestones and accomplishments as if they were your own and to be present in each other's lives during both the joyful moments and the challenging ones. I also emphasize the importance of spending time with friends—in person—creating shared experiences that become the heart and soul of our friendships. Yet, the book also compels you to confront the tough aspects of friendships, allowing you to recognize when dynamics become unhealthy and when you need to make difficult decisions to end them for your own well-being.

This book will help you navigate the complex and sometimes murky waters of adult friendships. Throughout the book, you will find actionable steps and reflection prompts that empower you to apply the **eight tenets** of a new **Framework of Dynamic Friendship** to your own life. I want you to be inspired to deepen your connections, overcome obstacles, and experience the true joy and fulfillment that come from friendships. *Friends Matter, for Life* is more than just a book; it lights a path to cultivating and maintaining friendships throughout life.

As we navigate this journey together, I must confess that the intricate dance of friendship sometimes eludes even me. I don't always have all the answers, and like anyone else, I stumble and seek guidance along the way. But one thing I'm certain about is that I can't fathom a world without the beauty of friendship. Writing this book became as essential to me as sharing it with you, because, let's face it, life is simply better with strong and meaningful connections.

In a world where unprecedented numbers of people wrestle with loneliness, friendship is profoundly urgent. We all have an innate need to be seen, understood, known—and loved. I believe friendships are the bedrock of connections, conduits for spreading love, fostering belonging, and facilitating mutual understanding that is healing and empowering.

Like it has done for me, I hope this book inspires you to grow new friendships and revere existing ones with a fresh perspective. May it empower you to embrace your friendships with genuine appreciation, nurture them intentionally, and build a legacy of enduring connections. Here's a simple truth: To have friends, you must first be a friend. As you embark on this journey, let the insights and reflections in these pages shape your friendships for the better. Remember, friends matter—for life.

With warmth and anticipation for your journey,

Kimberly

CHAPTER ONE

Introduction to Dynamic Friendship

In recent years, a remarkable discovery in medical research revealed that the quantity and quality of our friendships have a greater impact on our happiness, health, and even our risk of mortality than almost any other factor, second only to quitting smoking.[1]

Friends aren't just nice to have—they're vital. They serve as our lifeline, boosting our feel-good hormones like oxytocin,[2] reducing stress, and enhancing our overall health and well-being.[3][4] Satisfaction from our friendships is among the most reliable predictors of our overall life satisfaction.[1][4][5] Quality, however, not quantity, underpins this satisfaction.[4] The level of happiness we experience in our friendships is crucial in reaping their benefits.[6][7]

Regrettably, our society faces a pressing loneliness crisis, despite our undeniable need for human connection.[8] Loneliness is that uncomfortable feeling we experience when we think our social life isn't as full or as meaningful as we want it to be; we perceive that we don't have enough friends or the ones we have aren't really connecting with us in a deep way.[9] It's a strange paradox, isn't it? In a world more connected than ever through the Internet and social media, so many people are grappling with feelings of loneliness. In fact, there's a strong correlation between increased feelings of loneliness and the use of social media to maintain relationships. [10] Our virtual focus has also led to a decrease in face-to-face interactions with our friends—social connections that are essential for forging deep, personal bonds. [9]

People often avoid discussing loneliness, as there's a lingering sense of shame in admitting loneliness in our highly "connected" world. A silent epidemic is taking root. Not surprisingly, even in the face of our undeniable need for human connection, friendships are under-researched and socially undervalued, possibly because of their increasing complexity over time. [11] Unlike romantic relationships and marriages, friendships don't follow an established script, or abide by specific laws or social norms. [12] But we can't let that be an excuse. After all, understanding the nature of friendship bonds might be the knowledge we need to break the chains of loneliness that so many people feel today. Being seen and understood by another is not just a luxury; it's a fundamental human necessity. Our quest for deep, personal connections is relentless because these bonds are proven to be one of the strongest predictors of happiness. This truth bears repeating: close, meaningful friendships are essential for our well-being. [13]

Still, we often prioritize other relationships while neglecting friendships. As we age, especially after the age of twenty-five, friendships tend to deteriorate rapidly and continue to decline throughout our lives. [12] In fact, nearly one-third of American adults have two or fewer friends. [15] Moreover, we are dedicating decreasing amounts of time to our friends—a meager three hours per week. [14] These statistics are unacceptable. Even as we age, we all need friends, perhaps even more so as we progress through life and its increasing complexities. [16] [17]

Building genuine friendships isn't a solo effort; it requires reciprocal commitment to being the kind of friend we desire. It involves investing time, energy, and the ability to grow together. As adults, we frequently navigate the complexities of our friendships without a clear guide. Balancing the comfort of old companions with the excitement of new connections is both fulfilling and challenging. Amid life's heavy demands, nurturing existing bonds and fostering new ones requires adaptability. In these pages, you'll discover the power within you to reshape or re-energize your friendship story, a power stemming from knowledge, introspection, and purposeful steps.

Empowering readers to reverse the trend of declining adult friendships, *Friends Matter, for Life* speaks to anyone who acknowledges the deep impact of friendships and wishes to cultivate stronger, more fulfilling relationships. If you are here in this moment, that is you—welcome to the beginning of your journey into dynamic friendship.

This book brings to light a new **Framework of Dynamic Friendship** to provoke reflection and encourage action, bringing together a range of insights to support each of its **eight tenets**. The eight tenets reflect key skills valued across many theories of human behavior, considered essential for nurturing strong and dynamic relationships. Here, the framework integrates these principles into a straightforward guide, helping you apply them to your friendships in a way that fits your unique circumstances and relationships. The framework's eight tenets, each acting as a pillar of support for rich and fulfilling friendships, set the foundation for the deeper exploration waiting in the chapters ahead.

So, let's dive into the meaning of friendship.

Friend, noun: Someone we know and cherish, and with whom we share a bond of mutual affection that goes beyond family or romance.[18]

Friendship, noun: The beautiful rollercoaster of emotions and actions shared between friends; the state of being connected as friends.[18]

People all around the globe recognize the treasure of friendship.[19] [20] [21] Yet, understanding and navigating friendships is sometimes quite a puzzle; people are complex, and so are our friendships.

What truly distinguishes dynamic friendships? In this book, "dynamic" is a unique play on two concepts. First, dynamic friendship means that friendships are continuously evolving and adapting, much like life itself. Second, it suggests that friendships have a powerful and significant influence on our lives. In a dynamic friendship, you're not merely existing side by side with another individual. You're actively participating in each other's lives, sharing experiences and aspirations, and creating a lively exchange of positive energy. Dynamic friendship is a type of friendship characterized by continuous growth, change, and adaptability. People actively engage in nurturing and evolving their relationships, adjusting to life's changes, and addressing challenges together. These friendships bring a unique sense of excitement and enrichment to our lives. As with life, friendships are not static; they shift, adjust, and adapt as people and circumstances evolve. It's in the navigation of these dynamics—through communication, trust, shared experiences, and personal growth—that we truly cultivate vital bonds.

This is where the Framework of Dynamic Friendship comes into play. Picture the framework as a compass, guiding you as you navigate the fluctuating landscape of friendships. The goal here isn't just to understand friendship dynamics but also to help you skillfully navigate them. The eight tenets of this approach include characteristics known to breathe life into our friendships: Recognizing various types of friends, mastering the art of sincere communication, accepting imperfections, blending our social circles, building trust, finding harmony in giving and receiving, knowing when to adjust or let go, and embarking on the empowering journey of self-compassion. By intentionally embracing these tenets, we forge deeper connections, overcome obstacles, and foster positive and supportive relationships with our cherished friends.

Within the pages of this book, the framework compels us to engage actively, reflect on ourselves, and adapt to the ever-changing nature of friendships. Remember, this framework isn't just words on a page; it's a practical guide to enhance your understanding of friendship, improve your friendship skills, and boost your overall well-being and happiness.

At its core, the Framework of Dynamic Friendship explores the following eight tenets that contribute to the vitality and growth of friendships:

1. **Recognizing:** A key aspect of nurturing dynamic friendship is the ability to recognize the different types of friends we have or desire to have, and their respective roles in our lives. By identifying and acknowledging our friendships based on compatibility, needs, and boundaries, we can better manage and cultivate meaningful connections.
2. **Communicating:** Effective communication serves as a cornerstone of strong friendships. It involves actively listening to our friends, expressing ourselves honestly and authentically, and genuinely understanding their perspectives and emotions. Through open and honest communication, we foster trust, empathy, and a deeper connection with those we cherish.
3. **Accepting:** Acceptance plays a critical role in dynamic friendship. This tenet entails embracing and appreciating the differences and imperfections of our friends. Understanding that no friendship is perfect, we navigate disappointments and conflicts with empathy, compassion, and a willingness to work through challenges. By practicing acceptance, we create an environment of

understanding and support where friendships can flourish.

4. **Blending:** This tenet sheds light on the significance and complexities of integrating friend groups, romantic partners, and family members. It explores the advantages and challenges that come with creating opportunities for social blending and experiencing diverse social contexts. By exploring the dynamics of blending, we gain a deeper understanding of how it can enrich our friendships while also navigating the potential challenges that may arise.
5. **Safeguarding:** Trust forms the foundation of strong friendships. It means being reliable, loyal, and having unwavering faith in our friends. Safeguarding goes hand in hand with trust, as it involves standing up for and supporting our friends when they face challenges or adversities, being their advocate and champion in times of need.
6. **Reciprocating:** Healthy friendships thrive on a balance of giving and receiving. Reciprocating in friendships isn't just about the kindness we extend, but also the warmth and support we are willing to receive. It's a dance of give-and-take that thrives on selflessness and a positive spirit. By actively participating in this exchange, we nurture friendships that are both giving and gracious, creating a dynamic where positivity flourishes and the bond deepens.
7. **Recalibrating:** Recognizing when to recalibrate or let go of a friendship is an essential aspect of the framework. It means assessing the health and value of a friendship and making decisions that promote personal growth

and well-being. Sometimes, it may be necessary to recalibrate the dynamics of the friendship or, in certain circumstances, to make the difficult choice of letting go for the sake of our own happiness and growth.

8. **Self-friending:** This tenet emphasizes the importance of self-care, self-reflection, and self-acceptance, and self-compassion in friendships. It encourages us to prioritize our own growth and develop a positive and nurturing relationship with ourselves. When we become better friends to ourselves, we enhance our ability to cultivate more meaningful connections with others.

These eight tenets lie at the heart of what truly makes friendships meaningful and dynamic. Given the complexity of human friendships, no single theory captures all of the nuances. The beauty of the Framework of Dynamic Friendship is that it integrates insights from various theories that uphold each of these tenets, offering a holistic view of friendship. The framework cohesively consolidates and organizes these concepts, making it easier for you to apply the framework in your own life. By incorporating and embracing these tenets, you can cultivate a foundation for vital, dynamic friendships that bring joy, fulfillment, and growth.

Consider the remarkable story of four friends: Anna, Rachel, Sarah, and Steph. As childhood friends from the same neighborhood, they established a powerful bond through countless shared experiences. Their laughter filled the air during summer pool parties as they exchanged secrets during sleepovers, passed notes during classes, and came to view each other's families as their own. They stood arm-in-arm through happy and tumultuous teenage milestones—first dates, first kisses, first cars, and other unforgettable "firsts" of youth. They were inseparable.

As high school ended, their individual paths led them to different colleges and cities. Anna opted for a path in healthcare, while Rachel found her calling in the meticulous world of accounting. Sarah ventured into the world of science, while Steph chose to nurture young minds as an educator. Though their chosen life paths diverged, their friendship served as a steadfast undercurrent that never wavered.

As they matured, they collectively experienced life's significant events, even if from afar—the births of children and the challenges of raising families, the excitement of new jobs and the stress of relocations, and even the shared grief over the separation and death of loved ones. They listened, they shared, they celebrated, and they empathized, ensuring that their childhood bond thrived amid the continuous changes that life presented. Even as each friend danced to the rhythm of her own life, they remained intertwined in each other's journeys. Each of them brought something unique to the table, and their individual qualities worked harmoniously to create a strong and lasting friendship. They often playfully joked about each person playing a specific role within their group dynamic—the boss, the realist, the witty one, and the feelings overseer. However, beneath the humor lay a grain of truth, as their distinct gifts and personalities truly served as pillars that upheld and strengthened their bond.

Though they never entirely lost touch, there were "gap years" during which distance and life's demands strained their communication and time spent together. Despite these distances, both physical and emotional, their loyalty to the friendship endured. Intent on eliminating any more gap years, they reignited their connection and became more deliberate in their communication, using phone calls, video chats, and lengthy text threads to share everything from mundane daily updates to significant life events. They also preserved an annual reunion tradition—a sacred, nonnegotiable ritual that held steadfast despite their busy schedules.

The path of their friendship wasn't always smooth, yet the thought of abandoning it never crossed their minds. Inevitable disagreements and conflicts arose, but they confronted these with open hearts, empathetic understanding, and respect for a bond that only a shared history can provide. They fiercely defended each other, as sisters would. They greeted celebrations with joy, as if they were still living a few doors away from each other. Their childhood friendship didn't just survive, it thrived and deepened into adulthood, fueled by their unwavering dedication and effort. Because of this friendship, they each became better individuals.

The story of Anna, Rachel, Sarah, and Steph stands as a beautiful testament to the enduring power of dynamic friendship. Their lifelong bond matures with time, embodying the fundamental tenets of the Framework of Dynamic Friendship. They master the art of recognizing, with each friend playing a unique and indispensable role, ensuring the stability of their relationship. Their open and continuous communication forges unbreakable bonds and provides unwavering support; they always find time for each other even when they lived worlds apart. Acceptance serves as the cornerstone of their friendship, adapting to differences and embracing imperfections. The blending of their families enriches their lives, creating a tapestry of shared experiences and memories. Trust forms their foundation, ensuring the durability of their bond, while safeguarding against external threats is always a collective effort. Their friendship maintains a balance of giving and receiving, embracing reciprocal warmth and support, even when it's challenging to ask for or accept help. They've become adept at recalibrating when necessary, acknowledging that even in the best of friendships, there are moments when some adjustments are needed to let fresh air flow into their connection. As important, their individual journeys of self-awareness over the years ensure they have the energy and love needed to nurture this extraordinary bond. Their bond, still robust after more than fifty years, serves as a reminder of a simple, yet profound truth—friends matter, for life.

As we dive into the forthcoming chapters, you'll discover a wealth of wisdom and actionable advice. Each chapter addresses one of the framework's eight tenets, accompanied by several recommended **actions**, scenarios to **envision**, and thought-provoking **reflection prompts**. The prompts are thoughtfully crafted to ignite self-reflection and deepen your understanding of your current friendships, unlocking their immense potential for growth and fulfillment.

Navigating the intricacies of adult friendships can be challenging, and the prospect of stepping out of your comfort zone to do so may feel daunting. However, this book is here to guide you, offering insights and practical advice. If you seek more meaningful friendships, remember this: It's the steps taken, not the ones avoided, that will lead you to deep and rewarding relationships.

As you explore the book, focus on the tenets and actions that resonate most with you right now. You may not need or choose to apply all of them immediately, but you'll have a toolkit for when you do. Regardless of how you apply these tenets, wholeheartedly considering all of them and actively engaging with the prompts will empower you to forge stronger connections and weave a tapestry of truly meaningful friendships. Friendships are diverse and take various forms influenced by culture, personal preferences, and societal factors. Adapt and personalize the framework to your unique experiences and relationships. Get ready for an enlightening journey ahead, one that rewards your active commitment of time and energy to nurturing invaluable relationships.

By the time you reach the end of this book, you will:

1. Embrace a richer understanding of dynamic friendships and their transformative impact on your life.
2. Master the Framework of Dynamic Friendship and its eight essential tenets that shape meaningful connections.
3. Apply each tenet to breathe new life into every friendship.
4. Gain practical strategies that bring the tenets to life in your daily interactions.
5. Engage with reflections that deepen self-awareness and shed light on the breadth and depth of your friendships.
6. Tailor the framework to your unique life story, strengthening the bonds you share with others.
7. Step confidently onto a path of creating and nurturing friendships that grow and flourish with you.

PART I

Foundational Tenets

CHAPTER TWO

Recognizing

Adding one more friend to your circle can significantly boost your overall health—in fact, a nearly seven percent improvement; the richer your social network, the more advantageous friendship becomes for your overall wellness. [1]

Recognizing in the context of friendship means understanding how we identify and acknowledge the incredible variety of friends that can enrich our life. Identifying involves understanding the different types of friendships that exist in our lives, based on depth of connection, shared interests, and emotional intimacy. Acknowledging allows us to mentally sort and categorize our friendships, set boundaries, and manage expectations within each relationship.

This process of recognition is not just about appreciating friends for what they offer but also assessing our friendship needs. It encourages us to examine our social circle critically, identifying gaps where new friends could enrich our lives or where existing relationships could be deepened. By evaluating our friendships, we can recognize which ones provide support, challenge us, or help us grow, and which areas of our social needs may be unmet.

Every friendship brings distinct gifts and unique additions to your world, whether it's a friend who fills your life with laughter, one who infuses a sense of adventure, or another who provides a profound emotional connection. Understanding this helps us to not only appreciate the existing bonds but also to seek out new connections that address different facets of our friendship needs.

Recognizing your friendships allows you to navigate your social relationships with newfound ease and foster deeper bonds that resonate with your innermost self.

Making friends is like upgrading how healthy you are—it doesn't just feel good, it can also make you healthier and help you live longer.[3] [4] Take your time with each of these actions, envision the possibilities, and reflect. In this chapter, you will uncover the innate strength and power within you to identify the connections that add value to your life in ways you might not have thought possible.

1. **Welcome the range.** Understand that friendships aren't one-dimensional; they vary in depth and engagement, but all are valuable. From casual interactions with a neighbor to profound connections with lifelong companions, each bond has its unique essence. You might find camaraderie with a colleague, bond over shared hobbies with someone from a club, or even discover friendship within your extended family. These relationships can span across age groups, cultures, and personal histories. Embracing this range allows you to navigate different facets of your life with companionship and shared understanding. By welcoming friendships in all their forms, you can build a rich mosaic of meaningful connections and shared moments that enhance every facet of your life.

- **Envision:** You and your workout partner, who you've come to know over the past few months, regularly enjoy a post-workout morning coffee at a nearby café. Bonded by a shared passion for fitness, you have become each other's accountability allies, motivating one another to stay on track with your fitness goals. They may not be the person you confide your deepest emotions to, but their presence brings a sense of camaraderie and support to your gym routine, making it more enjoyable and rewarding. In contrast, there's your childhood best friend who has been by your side since kindergarten. You've shared countless memories together, from having fun on your school playground to navigating the ups and downs of adolescence and adulthood. This friend knows you inside out and has been your unwavering pillar of support through thick and thin. You share an unbreakable bond that feels like family. Embracing the fact that these two friendships are distinct in their dynamics, you recognize that each plays a unique and valuable role in enhancing your overall social well-being right now.

- **Reflect:** Think through the different types of friendships in your life. Consider the range of closeness and connections they offer. Taken together, how do these friendships contribute to your overall social well-being? Think about the specific joys and advantages that each type of friendship brings. How can you further embrace and appreciate the different friendships you have? Explore ways to nurture both your casual acquaintances and your deep, long-lasting friendships, allowing them to thrive and enrich your life.

2. **Stay open.** Whether you've spent your entire life in one place or been a bit of a nomad, always leave room for new friendships to find you. Keep your heart open and attuned to those serendipitous moments when new friendships come knocking. Building close bonds isn't restricted by age or life stage; sometimes, the most cherished connections happen when you least expect them. Additionally, people may enter your life briefly but leave a lasting imprint. Whether you're relishing the energy of youth or embracing the wisdom of your golden years, fresh connections can breathe new life into your world at any moment. Pay attention to those instances when you meet someone and instantly sense a unique connection—a spark that ignites the possibility of a profound friendship. Step out of your comfort zone and initiate a date! These encounters might hold the missing pieces you didn't even know were absent from other relationships. So, embrace the chance to form meaningful bonds, and remember that every age is ripe for new friendships. Your openness and willingness to take the risk and invest will pave the way for friendships that bring extraordinary joy and depth to your life journey.

- **Envision:** You enroll in a weekly local community art class to stimulate your creativity. As you engage in conversations and collaborate on class projects, you sense a unique connection with another student. There is an immediate understanding and appreciation for each other's artistic styles, ideas, and feedback. Overcoming a tinge of awkwardness, you extend an invitation to go to a movie. As time goes by, your interactions outside the art class grow, and you find yourselves spending more time together, exploring art galleries, attending workshops, and venturing out to other inspiring art-related outings. Your bond transcends beyond art discussions, as you begin to share personal stories, dreams, and aspirations. What started as a casual acquaintance in the art class now holds the promise of a lifelong friendship built on the solid foundation of mutual artistic understanding and shared passions. Your shared love for creativity not only adds depth and joy to your artistic pursuits but also creates a meaningful and enduring friendship that enriches both your lives in profound, unexpected ways. This friendship becomes a source of inspiration and encouragement. It is also a reminder that the power of shared passions can forge lifelong bonds.

- **Reflect:** Consider the friendships you've developed throughout your life. Can you recall instances where you felt a special connection with someone and wished to nurture it further? What factors may have held you back from pursuing those friendships more actively? Consider the steps you can take to improve these connections and transform them into meaningful relationships. Do you put yourself in situations to meet new friends? If not, why not? Embrace the excitement and endless possibilities that come with cultivating friendships at any stage of life.

3. **Break the age-gender norms.** Forge meaningful friendships regardless of what society says about age, gender, or anything else. Intergenerational friendships break down barriers, offering fresh perspectives and mutual learning across generations. These

relationships provide opportunities for older friends to share wisdom while younger friends infuse energy and new perspectives. Challenging gender norms allows connections to form based on shared values rather than labels, fostering understanding and dismantling stereotypes. Contrary to the myth that males and females can't be friends, mixed-gender friendships offer unique opportunities for diverse perspectives, emotional support, and personal growth. By embracing these less typical connections, we tap into the essence of genuine rapport. So, challenge societal norms. Seek friendships based on shared passions, aspirations, and compatibility rather than constraints. The value of a friendship lies not in age or gender but in the authenticity of the connection and the growth it brings.

- **Envision:** Picture yourself going to a hiking meetup. When you arrive, there's a diverse group of people spanning a range of ages and genders, all gathered at the trailhead. Most of them happen to be several years older than you. Initially uncertain if you'll fit in, you embark on the adventure together, and something remarkable occurs. As you hike, age and gender seem to fade into the background, replaced by a mutual passion for the great outdoors. The camaraderie that forms during this excursion leads to an unexpected invitation to join their hiking club, and your fellow hikers quickly transform into your close-knit community. Together, you soon provide each other with mutual support, share laughter, and form a bond over your mutual love for nature and hiking. These diverse friendships open up new dimensions of experiencing the world, broaden your perspectives, provide an unmet need for mentoring—all because you dared to defy societal expectations.

- **Reflect:** Think about your friendships that have defied societal norms around age and gender. How have these relationships enhanced your life and broadened your horizons? Have you ever hesitated to form friendships with people who differ in age or gender due to societal pressures? Consider the richness and growth that comes from embracing diverse friendships. How can you actively seek out and nurture connections that break free from preconceived notions and embrace the beauty of friendships that transcend age and gender?

4. **Mix it up.** While it's natural to gravitate toward forming friendships with those who share similar backgrounds, interests, or perspectives, it's also enriching to diversify your circle. Embrace the opportunity to learn and grow from friendships with people who bring different experiences and viewpoints into your life. While familiarity can provide comfort, think about the vast array of experiences and insights to be gained from relationships with people who differ from you. Variety is the spice of life, and friendships are no exception. If you want to add more "spice" to your life, be proactive in seeking out friendships with people from racial and ethnic backgrounds, cultures, sexual orientations, gender expressions, and economic statuses that may differ from your own. Intentionally diversifying your social circle can lead to fresh insights, unique experiences, and a more inclusive worldview. Ignite your spirit by

stepping into community celebrations, joining cultural alliances, participating in enlightening workshops, or simply gravitating toward activities that reflect your passions while also attracting a diverse range of people. Diverse friendships offer valuable opportunities for learning from others, challenging your own assumptions, and deepening understanding and appreciation for people from all walks of life.

- **Envision:** You receive an invitation to a multicultural potluck dinner organized by a close friend. As you walk into their home, you're greeted by the buzz of laughter and chatter. It's a diverse and vibrant crowd, representing various cultural backgrounds and life experiences. Though this is a new experience for you, you strike up conversations with different people, each with their own unique stories to share. You meet a woman who moved from India to pursue her dreams of becoming an entrepreneur, a man who grew up in Brazil and is passionate about sharing the beauty of his culture through dance, and a couple from Japan who are on a mission to promote eco-friendly practices. The gathering also offers a delightful journey of the senses as you sample a variety of international dishes, each representing the culinary artistry and cultural significance of the attendees. Through these experiences, you realize the immense value of friendship across cultures. You find yourself drawn to the beauty of connecting with people from different walks of life, enriching your understanding of the world. As the gathering comes to an end, you say your goodbyes with promises to keep in touch. You leave the gathering with a dinner date scheduled for next week with a newfound friend from Brazil, excited to continue building on the connections you made. The experience serves as a reminder that every encounter holds the potential for meaningful connections and new experiences.

- **Reflect:** Pause to reflect on the diversity within your current circle of friends. How many friends do you have who come from different backgrounds or cultures or who have different opinions and perspectives? Consider the benefits of having friends who are different from you. How have these friendships expanded your understanding of the world and contributed to your personal growth? Reflect on any hesitations or barriers you may have in forming friendships with people who are different from you and explore ways to overcome them. What steps can you take to actively seek out and embrace friendships with people who bring diverse perspectives, interests, and experiences into your life?

5. **Prioritize quality.** Keep in mind that having multitudes of friends doesn't necessarily equate to happiness. Instead, it sometimes leads to feeling overwhelmed and disconnected, especially if there is little depth. While some people are better at managing numerous friendships than others, fixating on the sheer quantity of friends can limit the time and energy you have to genuinely connect with each one. What really counts is the authentic value each friend brings to your life and the bond you share with them. And it's important to note

that prioritizing quality over quantity doesn't mean exclusively valuing long-term friendships; it's entirely possible to experience unique closeness with someone you only occasionally interact with. In essence, prioritize the quality of your friendships for a more fulfilling and enriching social life. This means nurturing the meaningful connections you have, whether they are with lifelong friends or acquaintances, as these are the relationships that truly add meaning to your life.

- **Envision:** Picture yourself with a lively social life, surrounded by numerous friends and acquaintances. Your calendar is packed with various social events and gatherings, from birthday parties for both children and adults, to weekly church or club meetings, to dinners and parties on the weekends. It seems like you have it all—a vibrant social scene and plenty of activities to keep you engaged. However, deep down, you can't shake a feeling of loneliness and a longing for more meaningful connections. In a powerful moment of self-reflection, you come to realize that the sheer number of friendships doesn't necessarily equate to true fulfillment. Determined to find genuine joy and purpose in your social interactions, you decide to take a step back and reevaluate your approach to friendships. Over the next two weekends, you make deliberate choices about which events and gatherings to attend. You opt for gatherings where you connect on a deeper level with like-minded people who share your passions and interests. As you embrace these intentional choices, you start to experience a shift in your social life. The loneliness you once felt begins to fade, replaced by a sense of belonging and fulfillment. Your calendar may have fewer social engagements, but each interaction becomes more meaningful and enriching. You discover that the true power of friendships lies in the quality of connections and shared experiences.

- **Reflect:** Recall the friendships in your life and the delicate balance between quantity and quality. How many close friends do you currently have? Are there multiple people whom you consider your best friends or close friends? What specific qualities or characteristics do you value most in a close friend? As you reflect on these traits, consider how they contribute to the authenticity of your relationships. Challenge the notion that a busy calendar, packed with people and events, equates to popularity or a sense of duty. Are there any adjustments you can make in your approach to friendships to create a more enriching and rewarding experience? Reassess the balance between the number of friends you have, as well as the importance of these connections, to pave the way for more fulfilling and authentic friendships that resonate with your values and bring genuine joy to your life.

6. **Laugh a little (or a lot).** Humor is a prized gift in friendship, and having a friend who not only laughs easily but also makes others laugh is a true delight. Their infectious laughter has the magical ability to transform ordinary moments into extraordinary memories, while their wit never fails to elicit smiles from everyone. It's like they carry

a pocketful of joy that they generously share with the world. Embrace the company of people who find humor in the simplest of things and have the remarkable knack for lifting spirits and infusing a room with their infectious laughter. These are the friends who sprinkle your life with happiness, creating an uplifting atmosphere in almost every encounter. Humorous friends are like a breath of fresh air, reminding us not to take everything so seriously all the time. These friends serve as a gentle reminder to reconnect with childlike glee. Let's face it—we all get caught up in being grown-ups, but sometimes we need to be playful and laugh at silly jokes!

- **Envision:** You have a small gathering for board game night at your home, filled with a group of close friends. Among them is that one friend with an extraordinary talent for effortlessly lighting up the room with their quick wit and uncanny way of drawing out people's playfulness. As the evening unfolds, someone suggests capturing the moment with photos; your witty friend takes this as an opportunity to infuse a dose of playful spontaneity. With their infectious enthusiasm, they propose a round of silly-face photo ops. At first, there's a moment of hesitation, but one by one, people embrace the idea, contorting their features into outrageous expressions, laughter erupting with each snapshot. The barriers of adulthood seem to fade away, filling the room with camaraderie and genuine smiles. As the evening winds down, you're left with a heart full of gratitude for this friend who, in a world often weighed down by responsibilities, reminds you all to infuse life with laughter and lightheartedness.

- **Reflect:** Think about the impact of humor and laughter in your friendships. Identify those friends who effortlessly bring laughter to your life, leaving you with aching cheeks and a happy heart. Consider ways to incorporate more levity and lightheartedness into your friendships. Can you identify any barriers or fears that may hinder your ability to embrace wit and humor? Explore strategies to cultivate a mindset that welcomes and appreciates friends who have a sense of humor. Are there any steps you can take to welcome more laughter into your relationships? Embrace the power of laughter, as laughter shared among friends has the remarkable ability to strengthen bonds, create lasting memories, and make life's journey all the more exhilarating.

7. **Entertain spontaneity.** Having spontaneous friends in your life adds a sprinkle of excitement and surprise, keeping friendships more vibrant and enjoyable. When friends engage in spontaneous activities together, it allows for a deeper level of connection, as both friends are willing to step out of their comfort zones and experience new things together. It's in these unscripted moments that friends often find their most cherished memories, disrupting the everyday routine with bursts of excitement. In our often overly scheduled lives, spontaneity allows for freedom from plans and expectations and offers space where friends can relish the present and the thrills of the unforeseen.

- **Envision:** Imagine that you are planning to have a relaxing weekend at home, watching movies and catching up on tasks. However, on a whim, your friend suggests going on a spontaneous road trip to a nearby beach town. Despite not being part of your original weekend plan, you decide to embrace the idea and go for it. You both pack your bags quickly, hop in the car, and hit the road. The spontaneity of the trip brings a sense of excitement and adventure, and you create unforgettable memories together, from exploring the quaint streets of the beach town to having impromptu beach picnics and watching the sunset. The spontaneous road trip not only reenergizes you but also deepens your friendship.

- **Reflect:** Think about a recent time when you embraced spontaneity with a friend. How did the experience make you feel? Did it enhance your connection with your friend? Reflect on the impact of spontaneity on your friendships. Are there times when you hesitated to be spontaneous in your friendships? If so, what prevents you from saying "yes"? Consider the benefits of being open to impromptu activities with your friends and how this openness can bring more excitement and joy into your life. What steps can you take to entertain spontaneity and incorporate more unplanned adventures with your friends?

8. **Set boundaries.** A boundary is like a friendly agreement about how you and your friends can support each other while also respecting

personal space and time. Setting boundaries with friends is sometimes necessary for preserving a healthy equilibrium in your friendships and personal life. For instance, friends may overstep by frequently asking for favors, intruding on your private time without notice, or expecting constant communication, all of which might necessitate setting clear boundaries. Boundaries help balance independence and togetherness in the relationship, prevent burnout and misunderstandings, and aid clear communication. Think of boundaries as guideposts that help you navigate your friendships while ensuring your well-being. Recognize that each friendship is unique, and the boundaries you set may vary based on the level of intimacy and dynamics involved or desired in the friendship. Openly and kindly communicating desired boundaries is a form of self-care and is crucial for developing deeper and more significant connections. When both parties understand and respect these boundaries, it leads to a more positive and balanced friendship where mutual respect and understanding flourish.

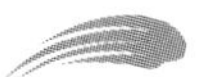

- **Envision:** You have a close friend who often calls you late at night, expecting you to be available for long conversations. While you value their friendship and don't want to let them down, you realize that it's affecting your sleep and overall well-being. A few days later, you call them at a reasonable hour, and in a kind way say: "Hey, I really value our friendship, and I love our late-night conversations. But, I've noticed that it's been affecting my sleep. Is there any chance we could find a different time during the day to connect? I want to make sure I give you my full attention and am at my best when we talk." By setting a boundary and kindly expressing your need for restful nights, you establish a healthier balance. You both find alternative times during the day to connect.

- **Reflect:** Examine the boundaries you have established within your friendships. Are they clear and effective in maintaining a healthy balance in your life? Consider the areas where you may need to set or reinforce boundaries to protect your well-being and maintain healthy dynamics in your friendships. How can you communicate your boundaries effectively while still serving open and supportive relationships? Reflect on the importance of evaluating your friendships and respecting the unique dynamics and levels of intimacy within each relationship.

9. **Cultivate personal and group connections.** Balance between group gatherings and one-on-one interactions. While group events and social gatherings are essential for building a sense of community, it's equally important to spend individual time with your friends. Focusing solely on group activities sometimes leads to unintentionally neglecting meaningful one-on-one connections and the ties that initiated these group relationships from the beginning. By acknowledging your time and interactions, you more effectively manage the varying demands of group and individual friendships, ensuring neither gets overshadowed. Just as you allocate time and energy to work, family, and personal interests, be sure to set aside this mutually beneficial quality time with individual friends. This way, you have a healthy equilibrium,

nurturing both group dynamics and the personal connections that deeply matter in your life.

- **Envision:** You have a close-knit group of friends who have been an integral part of your life for years. Despite your affection for each of them, you sometimes struggle to give the individualized attention they deserve—for a variety of reasons. While group gatherings are convenient, you know they sometimes miss the mark on personal connection. When you notice one friend in particular seems to be drifting away, you're moved to actively engage and bridge that growing gap. Trusting your instincts, you send a text to your friend: "Hey, how about we catch that new flick at the downtown cinema on Friday evening, just us two?" Their immediate response, filled with emojis and exclamation marks, confirms they're genuinely excited and appreciate the gesture. During your one-on-one outing, you find yourselves laughing and bonding like old times, dissolving any sense of distance that had crept in. You recognize that it's moments like these that reaffirm the irreplaceable value of individual connections, fortifying the ties that make your close-knit group truly extraordinary.

- **Reflect:** Consider how you currently manage your time among your various categories of friends. Are there instances where you may be inadvertently neglecting certain friendships or favoring one friend group over others? Consider the impact this may have on your relationships and overall satisfaction. How can you manage your time so that each friend feels cherished individually? Consider strategies that might easily fit into your routine, such as setting aside regular breakfasts or lunch catch-ups.

10. **Find your vibe.** Encountering new friends can happen organically, but more frequently, it takes intentional effort. Shared interests and passions can be powerful magnets that draw people together, creating an organic foundation for new friendships. Let what you love guide you to others. To discover compatible companions, start by exploring environments that align with your interests and passions. Attend workshops or classes to learn something new, explore cultural festivals, join clubs, attend social events. Use social media to learn about activities that genuinely excite you. If you're a book lover, consider joining a local book club or attending literary events. If fitness is your thing, sign up for exercise classes or group sports. Maybe you always wanted to try volunteering; look for opportunities to support causes close to your heart. By immersing yourself in these spaces, you'll naturally encounter people who share your enthusiasm and values. Don't be afraid to step out of your comfort zone. Trying new experiences or cultivating a variety of interests can pave the way for meaningful connections and enhance your overall well-being. Bear in mind that finding your vibe doesn't mean you'll instantly click with everyone you meet. But even if people don't share all your interests, unexpected connections can blossom when you least expect them.

- **Envision:** Let's say you have a passion for photography and want to connect with like-minded people. You take a leap and join a local photography club that meets monthly. In the club's workshops and photo walks, you engage in lively discussions about various techniques, equipment, and photo genres. The exchange of ideas flows effortlessly, and you realize how quickly you've become at ease with others who speak the same visual language. The bond you form with these new friends is different from any other connections you currently have in your life. It's a unique and profound camaraderie forged through shared passions and a mutual understanding of photography. You find yourself surrounded by a group of people who not only appreciate your creative vision but also inspire you to explore new horizons. Through these meaningful connections, your photography skills flourish, and these like-minded friends become more than just companions; they become a supportive and empowering tribe, adding a new and vibrant dimension to your life.

- **Reflect:** Take a moment to reflect on the yardstick you use to measure compatibility in your friendships. Are you consciously considering shared interests, values, and goals when forming new connections? How does this contribute to the strength of your existing friendships? Consider any missed opportunities or potential friendships you may have overlooked due to a lack of compatibility. How can you become more intentional in seeking out friendships with people who align with your values and interests? Consider how seeking compatibility and connections with like-minded people can cultivate more fulfilling and enriching friendships in your life.

11. **Embrace varying depths and duration.** Friendship depth varies—and that's perfectly okay. Not all friendships are meant to be deep and long-lasting. So, don't dismiss the value of casual connections. These could be the familiar faces you regularly bump into around your neighborhood or those with whom you frequently engage in friendly banter at the neighborhood bakery. There are also close friends who come into your life for brief periods, often tied to specific places or times. These friends can be like shooting stars—bright, intense, and unforgettable, even if they're fleeting. Whether they're college buddies, work colleagues, or someone in your daily car pool, their presence may be time-limited. Still, the experiences and memories you create together can be profound. The key here is to appreciate the friendship for what it is—a beautiful connection in a particular context. As life moves forward, your paths may diverge, but that doesn't diminish the meaning of the friendship during its time. These friends can teach you, support you, and offer unique perspectives. Be open to these encounters because, sometimes, they're the missing puzzle piece that completes a moment in your life. Understanding and acknowledging these various levels of friendship depth helps you manage your expectations. It's perfectly acceptable to have friends at different levels, as each serves a unique purpose and enriches your life in its own way. Take pleasure in the qualities they bring, whether they are casual acquaintances, close friends, or

somewhere in between. Rather than mourning the end of these friendships, celebrate the memories, lessons, and personal growth they contributed. They've played a role in your life story, enriching it with a presence and influence that resonates throughout your life's narrative.

- **Envision:** See yourself in your neighborhood, where one friendly neighbor stands out. You often exchange greetings and chat whenever you cross paths at your mailbox. These casual interactions bring a touch of warmth and contribute to a strong sense of community. You engage in light conversations about the weather, local events, or your pets, creating a friendly and familiar atmosphere. While this friendship may never move past a more surface level, it still adds a positive and comforting element to your everyday life. Contrast that with a work colleague who goes beyond being just a coworker. This colleague has become a close friend, even though your interactions primarily take place in the workplace over lunch or a cup of coffee. They are someone you rely on, confide in, and share both personal and professional thoughts with. Their presence not only enhances your work environment but also adds a sense of camaraderie and support to your daily interactions. Despite the confines of the office, this friendship significantly contributes to making your work a better place. These two contrasting friendship depths, both situational, remind us that each serves a unique purpose and enriches our lives in its own way.

- **Reflect:** Think on your expectations and perceptions of depth in friendships. Can you recognize and appreciate the varying levels of connection and longevity in your friendships? Consider the lessons and experiences you have gained from both casual and profound friendships. Are there any adjustments you need to make in terms of your expectations or the efforts you invest in different types of friendships? Reflect on the value and depth that each level of friendship brings to your life and how each contributes to your overall well-being.

12. **Cherish lifelong bonds.** Lifelong friendships are truly precious and deserve to be treated like the treasures they are. If you're fortunate enough to have such enduring connections, make a conscious effort to put your all into them. The longevity of these friendships should not be an excuse for complacency. Long-standing friendships should not be taken for granted. Instead of becoming content due to the duration of the relationship, see the history you share as a reason to invest even more effort and care into these bonds. If you have a best friend who stands the test of time, prioritize their friendship. Nurturing these beloved connections is essential for maintaining their strength and ensuring that they continue to enrich your life for years to come.

- **Envision:** Visualize a lifelong best friend, the one who's been your unwavering companion through all of life's ups and downs, sharing moments of joy, consoling you in times of sorrow, and creating lasting memories together. You recognize the profound significance of this enduring friendship and actively set aside quality time to connect with them at least once a month. Whether it involves a leisurely walk or a heartfelt conversation over the phone or through a video call, these moments are invaluable. Sometimes, when you connect it means offering a compassionate ear and a comforting presence during tough times, while at other times, it's simply about relishing each other's company, sharing laughter, or discussing the mundane aspects of life. Regardless of the particular activity, each instance spent together serves as a precious reminder of the deep and cherished bond you share.

- **Reflect:** Focus on any long-term friendships you have in your life. Reflect on how much time, energy, and support you have invested in these friendships. How have these extraordinary bonds enriched your life and brought you joy, comfort, and a sense of belonging? Consider the ways you can continue nurturing and cherishing these special connections in action. Are there gestures or acts of gratitude you can express to your lifelong best friends to show your love and appreciation? Could you do better? Reflect on the deep significance that these friendships hold and how they contribute to your overall happiness and well-being.

Recognizing friendship is about finding your tribe and your vibe, setting boundaries (and loosening the rigid ones if needed), and striking a balance that brings joy and fulfillment to your life. By embracing compatibility, forging healthy boundaries, and proactively seeking diverse friendships, you can weave a resilient and enriching social fabric that elevates your life's path. So, embrace the connections that resonate with your heart, even if they have just emerged; relish those lifelong best friendships; and always remember to prioritize the friendships that light up your world. Be open to the idea that friendship takes unexpected forms and blossoms in unanticipated places, enriching your life with their unique perspectives and experiences. And, remember, maintaining existing—and discovering new—friendships is an active, not passive, process. If you seek new friendships, venturing out of your usual routine to meet new people can be the first step toward forging some of the most exciting and rewarding relationships life has to offer.

CHAPTER THREE

Communicating

In the absence of open and heartfelt communication—actively reaching out to share your heart and mind with another person—our inner selves remain hidden, creating a barrier to understanding, and inhibiting the deep, caring feelings vital for growing close and meaningful friendships. [1]

When it comes to dynamic friendship, effective communication is the lifeblood that keeps our relationships strong, healthy, and deeply meaningful.[2] In this chapter, we shine a spotlight on the power of authentic and open communication as we explore its crucial role in nurturing our friendships. Effective communication is essential in all its forms. Without such open expression—the genuine act of sharing our deepest feelings and thoughts—we risk becoming secluded, our authentic selves masked and isolated.[1] Trust flourishes, understanding deepens, and connections grow stronger in an environment where communication is valued and prioritized. Opening ourselves up, expressing our thoughts and feelings freely, without expecting our friends to read between the lines, is one of the keys to enriching and sustaining our friendships.[3]

All that said, the art of communication is a hurdle for many. While some people may effortlessly convey their thoughts and feelings, others find it more difficult. Regardless of where you stand on the communication continuum, communication requires deliberate effort and ongoing practice. Even within our most cherished and enduring relationships, nurturing this skill is pivotal. In the pages that follow, we'll take a look at some nuances of genuine acts of communication and dialogue and offer insights and tools to bridge the gaps and amplify the joys that come with truly understanding and being understood by our friends.

1. **Keep it real.** Authentic communication is the bedrock of any strong relationship. Being authentic means being true to yourself and others in your conversations. Make it a priority to be open, honest, and genuine, freely sharing your thoughts, feelings, and experiences without hiding or pretending. Cultivate an environment where both you and your friends feel safe expressing yourselves without fear of judgment or criticism. Ultimately, insincere remarks damage both you and the bonds you share with friends, and over time, such insincerity becomes evident as people can see through it. Authenticity in communication allows for deeper connections and a stronger sense of trust between friends.

- **Envision:** Picture a scenario where you recently had a heart-to-heart talk with your friend over dinner about some concerns you have about their new romantic interest. The talk leads to a clash of opinions, and in the aftermath, a palpable tension in the air. Since then, an unsettling silence has hung between the two of you. Instead of allowing this discomfort to fester or pretending like it never happened, you decide to take the initiative to address it. You call your friend. When they answer, you speak from the heart: "I've been giving our last conversation a lot of thought. Our friendship means so much to me, and I think it's important that we address what happened. I felt some tension. Can we talk about it?" This vulnerable step sets the stage for an honest dialogue. Your friend, too, senses your authenticity and agrees. As you both share your thoughts and feelings, you not only resolve the issue but also strengthen trust and understanding within your friendship.

- **Reflect:** Recall your recent interactions with friends. Have there been instances where you held back your true thoughts or feelings? Reflect on why you hesitated to be authentic in those situations. Consider how being open and honest led to a deeper understanding and connection with your friends. Challenge yourself to have a genuine and heartfelt conversation with a friend about something that matters to you. Embrace vulnerability and transparency in your communication, knowing that it leads to more meaningful and fulfilling friendships.

2. **Tune into your habits.** Building and nurturing friendships requires consistent communication and a genuine interest in each other's lives. Consciously refine your communication practices to strengthen your friendships. While face-to-face interactions hold significant value, the essence of nurturing these bonds often lies in thoughtful efforts to maintain connection and show your friends they are appreciated. Small, consistent actions—like sending a text or making a call—can mean as much as grand gestures. Awareness and

intention in how and when you reach out can significantly enhance the depth and strength of your relationships. Commit to these habits with mindfulness, and you'll build a foundation of mutual appreciation and enduring connection.

- **Envision:** Every Friday, you make it a habit to send a warm text message to your friend who lives several hours away, checking in on how their week went and sharing a positive or interesting experience from your own life. Your message often includes a funny meme that made you laugh, a memory photo of the two of you, or a simple message expressing how much their friendship means to you or how much you admire certain qualities in them. Your most recent message simply said: "This photo of today's sunset made me think about your bright smile." Your friend responds with gratitude, saying that these small gestures always brighten their day and make them feel connected to you, even during busy times. "Thank you so much for your thoughtful messages, they truly make my week brighter! That sunset photo you sent was breathtaking, and it's incredible how, even from afar, I feel like we're sharing these beautiful moments together. Your friendship means the world to me too!" This regular exchange of positive messages fosters a deeper bond and a sense of warmth that strengthens your friendship over time.

- **Reflect:** Consider your current communication habits with your friends. How often do you reach out to them?

Are there any opportunities to incorporate simple gestures into your communication routine? Where could you improve? Consider the impact of these small acts of thoughtfulness in nurturing your friendships. Do you find creative ways to stay connected and make your friends smile? Think about how these actions can strengthen the bonds of friendship and create moments of joy and shared nostalgia.

3. **Understand that life happens.** Life can get busy, and it's normal for friends to go through periods of limited contact. Reconnecting may take time, and that's okay. Instead of assuming that their silence is about you, give them the benefit of the doubt and be patient. You may go months or years without connecting with a friend—this is not cause for dismissal. Just because you haven't connected in a while doesn't mean the friendship is no longer valid or that it never was. Maintain an open mindset and be willing to reconnect when the opportunity arises. Trust that when the time is right, you'll pick up where you left off.

- **Envision:** A professional meeting takes you to a city where a childhood friend lives whom you haven't spoken to in ages. Feeling a bit uncomfortable, you draft an email reaching out: "I'll be in your city next week for a conference. It's been far too long, and I really regret that we've let the years slip by without keeping in touch. Would you be up for meeting for dinner while I'm there?

I'd love to catch up and hear about what you've been up to." Your friend responds to your email, and you both acknowledge that life has been busy and express genuine regret for the time lost without being in each other's lives. Later that week, feeling a combination of nervousness and excitement, you meet for drinks, and as soon as you see each other, there's an instant connection again. The years apart seem to vanish as you reminisce about old memories. The laughter, understanding, and shared experiences reaffirm the special bond you once had and ignite a sense of excitement for the future of your rekindled friendship. You both express a desire to make the most of your future interactions, cherishing the opportunity to continue strengthening your connection.

- **Reflect:** Mull over your mindset when it comes to reconnecting with old friends. How do you typically react when you haven't been in touch for a while? Do you tend to dwell on the time lost and express regret, or do you focus on the potential of the future? Consider the factors that may contribute to the lack of communication, such as distance or life circumstances and how you can be more open to reconnecting when the opportunity arises. Remember, friendships can withstand the test of time and distance if we approach them with understanding, regret for the time lost, and a genuine desire to create new, meaningful moments together.

4. **Don't jump to conclusions.** As difficult as it is sometimes, avoid making assumptions if close friends become distant or silent for a while. Chances are that their lack of communication is not a reflection of their feelings toward you but rather a result of their own personal challenges or busy lives. It's important to remember that everyone has their ups and downs, and sometimes people's emotional tanks might simply bottom out. Instead of automatically assuming the worst, take the approach of open and honest communication. If you notice a change in their behavior or a lack of contact, consider reaching out to them directly and asking if everything is okay. This simple and sincere question can clear up any misunderstandings and pave the way for more meaningful conversations.

- **Envision:** Your friend hasn't replied to your last text messages for several days. Rather than jumping to the conclusion that they're ignoring or "ghosting" you, you take a moment to reflect and decide to reach out to them again, leaving a warm voice message: "Hi, I noticed we haven't talked in a while. I just wanted to check in and make sure everything is okay. I'm here for you if you need someone to talk to or if there's anything I can do to support you." To your surprise, your friend texts you later that day with sincere appreciation and opens up about the challenges they've been facing lately. Your willingness to communicate openly has strengthened your friendship and provided much-needed support for your friend.

- **Reflect:** Examine your reactions when you don't hear from friends. How do you typically interpret the silence of your friends? Do you tend to assume it's about you or take it personally? Reflect on the importance of avoiding assumptions and recognizing that people have their own lives and challenges. How can you reframe your perspective to not internalize a friend's silence?

5. **Give your best effort.** Acknowledge that nurturing a friendship requires a mutual commitment, where both individuals actively contribute to its growth. Effective communication is a cornerstone of this process. However, be aware that people have different communication styles. If you have a friend who is less likely to initiate, be willing to step up when needed to maintain the bond. Don't hesitate to be the one who reaches out first, organizes get-togethers, or keeps the conversation going. These efforts are valuable expressions of your investment in the friendship. If you're willing to invest effort into sustaining the friendship, it can thrive. While it's important not to keep a scorecard, pay attention to how you feel about the efforts you're making. When initiating contact feels forced or resentment begins to build, it's time to reassess the balance in your friendship.

- **Envision:** Imagine a scenario where you and your close friend used to have regular concert dates, but lately, they haven't been initiating any plans and neither have you. Feeling the need to reconnect, you take the lead and send them a heartfelt text message, "Hey there. It's been a while since we hit our favorite music venue, and I've really missed our nights out. How about we look for a show this Saturday? I'd love to hear about what's been going on in your life and share what's been happening with me, too. Let me know if that works for you. Looking forward to catching up and spending some quality time together!" Your friend responds enthusiastically right away, expressing their excitement to meet up. The spontaneity of your initiative sparks a smile for both of you and rekindles the connection you share.

- **Reflect:** Think about your willingness to put in effort for your friendships: How comfortable are you with taking the lead in maintaining the communication and connection with your friends? Are you willing to do most of the work if necessary? Do you keep a scorecard of who initiates more? Consider the importance of reciprocity in friendships and how you can strike a balance between initiating contact and expecting effort from your friends.

6. **Show genuine curiosity.** Letting your friends know that you are sincerely interested in their lives, whether you've known them for months or decades, is an aspect of friendship not to be underestimated. Take the time to inquire about their families, their hobbies, their pets, their aspirations and dreams, or simply inquire about their day. Engage in meaningful conversations, actively listening to their thoughts and feelings. Expressing sincere curiosity and care

for their well-being not only strengthens the emotional bond between you, it solidifies feelings of closeness and deepens the meaningful connection, making your relationship more authentic. People have a fundamental need to feel seen, heard, and understood by someone in their lives, and showing genuine interest in your friends is one way to meet this need.

- **Envision:** You have a friend you've known for a while, yet one day it strikes you that you're unfamiliar with the details of their everyday life. Over a relaxed coffee catch-up at the cozy corner café you both love, you strike up a conversation with your friend, intent on enhancing your knowledge of their daily life. You ask: "So, what have you been up to lately? Any new hobbies or projects? I realize I don't know much about your day-to-day, and I want to hear more about what's been filling your days." To your surprise, they reveal a newfound passion for bird watching. This revelation sparks genuine curiosity and excitement within you. Eagerly, you suggest setting aside a day for a shared birding adventure. Their face lights up. In making this gesture, you not only express genuine interest in their life but also deepen your understanding of their evolving character. Moreover, it presents an opportunity for both of you to learn and grow, and enriches your friendship on many levels.

- **Reflect:** Consider how curious you are about your friends. Do you actively inquire about their lives, their families, interests or preferences, and experiences?

Reflect on the impact of demonstrating curiosity and actively seeking to understand them better. Think about how to be more curious in your friendships and how to create more opportunities to connect on a deeper level. Are there ways you can show more genuine interest in your friends' lives?

7. **Choose your words wisely.** Be mindful of the impact your words have on your friends and choose them wisely, especially in situations where your words might carry significant weight or emotional impact. Assess which approach—candor or reserve—is best in the moment by considering factors like the sensitivity of the topic, your friend's emotional state, past experiences, intended outcomes, and the overall context. While honesty is important, opt for a gentle and thoughtful choice of words when addressing delicate subjects or discussing matters of great importance. Understanding when to use each approach is vital for effective communication and maintaining healthy, supportive friendships.

- **Envision:** Think about a situation where your friend excitedly shared their new business idea with you—they plan to purchase a food truck. As they share the details over the phone, you notice some potential challenges that they may face. But you also recognize their passion and enthusiasm, so you lead with genuine support and encouragement, saying, "Wow, I'm really impressed with your ambition and business savvy. It's clear how passionate you are about it, and I believe in your abilities to make it a success. If you ever want to bounce ideas off me or need any help, I'm here for you. I can't wait to see what happens next." By choosing your words wisely, you express both your support and your willingness to provide constructive input, leading to a positive and empowering conversation with your friend.

- **Reflect:** Recall your past interactions with your friends. Have there been instances where your words have unintentionally hurt or discouraged them? It's important to be mindful and sensitive to their feelings when communicating. Consider how you can improve your approach by finding the right balance between honesty and kindness. Remember, the way you choose your words can deeply impact your friendships, influencing the level of trust and support within them.

8. **Open up and be vulnerable.** Embrace the courage to share your thoughts, feelings, and experiences with your friends, and let them know when you need a listening ear. Being willing to be vulnerable and inviting them into your world creates a safe and supportive space for deeper connections and trust to flourish. It's important to acknowledge that feeling safe enough to open up can be tough for some people, and that's okay. Vulnerability feels like an act of bravery for many people, taking practice and effort. Remember, being open and genuine improves intimacy and strengthens the bond between friends. Of course, being vulnerable is a personal choice, and it's important to honor your feelings and boundaries. But, with

someone you trust, the more you show your authentic self, the more you encourage your friends to do the same—which leads to deeper and more meaningful friendships.

- **Envision:** Lately, the weight of work deadlines and personal obligations has been pressing down on you, leaving you feeling like you're constantly gasping for air. It's all become too much, yet you've kept it bottled up inside. Trusting in the strength of your bond, you reach out to a close friend to confide in, choosing the quiet comfort of your living room for the conversation. You share, "Lately, I've been feeling really overwhelmed with family, work, and personal commitments. It's been tough, but I'm grateful to have you as a friend to lean on. Would it be okay if I just vented for a bit?" Your friend listens with empathy, offering a comforting presence. Through this act of vulnerability, not only does your bond deepen but you feel the instant relief of unburdening to someone who understands.

- **Reflect:** Consider your past experiences with vulnerability in friendships. Have there been moments when you found it challenging to open up and share your thoughts, feelings, or experiences? Reflect on the impact of embracing vulnerability and sharing your authentic self with a friend. Notice the level of trust and connection that grew as a result of being open. Consider how your own willingness to be vulnerable influences the comfort level of your friends in sharing their thoughts and feelings with you. Embrace vulnerability to build meaningful and fulfilling relationships and create a safe space for others to be vulnerable with you.

9. **Spread the love.** Love is a fundamental emotional need. Let your friends know how much they mean to you and how grateful you are to have them in your life. Make it a point to tell your friends you love them, recognizing that love is received and felt differently by each person. Whether it's through heartfelt compliments, acts of kindness, encouraging words, or saying "I love you," ensure that your expressions of love are communicated in ways that truly connect with your friends. Even if they do not respond in kind or initially seem to downplay such gestures, your expressions of love and affection are crucial. When people feel loved, they often feel inspired and supported to take risks, grow, and explore new paths—isn't that what we want for our friends? Over time, these consistent words or acts of care will weave themselves into the fabric of your friendships, greatly enhancing their quality and bringing a richer sense of fulfillment to both you and your friends. Celebrate the love you share, for it is these connections that encourage us to strive for the best in ourselves and for each other.

- **Envision:** You and your friend are having dinner at a restaurant, catching up after a busy few months without seeing each other. As you share stories and laughter, a surge of appreciation washes over you. You suddenly feel overwhelmed by gratitude for their presence in your life.

Before parting ways, you take a moment to express your feelings sincerely: "I just want you to know how much I appreciate our friendship and how grateful I am to have you in my life," you say with a warm smile. Your friend does not respond with the same exact sentiment, but you part with a heartfelt hug, the kind that says everything words can't. The exchange strengthens a sense of warmth between you.

- **Reflect:** Consider how often you express love and affection to your friends. Are you comfortable telling or showing them that you care for and love them, even if they don't reply in the same way or deflect the sentiment? Reflect on the significance of expressing your care and appreciation for your friends and on how it contributes to the strength of your friendships. How can you incorporate more expressions of love into your interactions, making them a natural part of your friendship journey?

10. **Connect physically.** Consider the significance of physical touch in your friendships. Whether it's a warm hug, a congratulatory high five, or a comforting pat on the back, these gestures can convey warmth, support, and affection. Hugging, for instance, does wonders for your mood because it amps up serotonin, that feel-good hormone in your brain.[4] When serotonin is flowing, you're in your happy, calm, and confident zone. But when it's missing, well, your mood can take a hit. So, think about physical touch as a natural mood booster. One caveat—always remember to ensure that any

form of physical contact is consensual and appropriate for the specific relationship. Cultural norms and customs vary worldwide, and what might be seen as a friendly gesture in one culture could be perceived differently in another. Some people may feel uncomfortable or offended by certain forms of physical contact, while others may warmly embrace it. When both parties are receptive and comfortable, the simple act of physical touch strengthens the connection between friends and elevates overall well-being.

- **Envision:** See yourself sitting on a park bench with your friend, engrossed in a deep conversation where they share a vulnerable moment about a recent struggle with their spouse. You see the emotions in their eyes, and, instinctively, you reach out and place a comforting hand on their shoulder, letting them know you're there to offer support and empathy. Your touch conveys a sense of reassurance and understanding, deepening the emotional connection between the two of you. As your friend leans into the touch, you feel the trust between you growing stronger; they know they can rely on you in times of need. Your simple gesture of physical comfort speaks volumes about the depth of your friendship and creates a safe space for them to be vulnerable and share feelings openly.

- **Reflect:** Sit with your own feelings about physical contact within your friendships. How do you generally perceive physical touch, such as hugging, when it comes to your friendships? Are you open to embracing opportunities for appropriate physical contact and comfort when the situation calls for it? Take into account your cultural background, personal boundaries, and the concept of consent in any physical interactions. Reflect on the significant role that physical touch plays in conveying support, comfort, and a sense of closeness in friendships. How can you prioritize physical affection in your friendships while also being respectful of the boundaries and preferences of others?

11. **Embrace technology as a bridge.** Remember, engaging in direct in-person social interactions can significantly diminish feelings of loneliness. Yet, technology should not be overlooked—it can be a powerful instrument in preserving friendship ties if used thoughtfully within a broader communication strategy. Technology and online connections are especially valuable for those who find face-to-face socializing challenging or have an illness or disability that restricts mobility. Through social media, messaging apps, and video calls, we break down geographical barriers, allowing us to maintain real-time connections with friends. These digital tools enable us to share daily moments, celebrate achievements, and offer support, allowing a sense of closeness even when physical distance separates us. Online groups also offer opportunities for mutual activities, hobbies, and games, enriching our interactions. In best-case scenarios, technology should complement in-person interactions. Used as a tool to bridge connection gaps, it is invaluable for nurturing and sustaining friendships in our fast-paced lives.

- **Envision:** You recently became a member of an online fitness community and discovered that several other members live in your city. After some initial interactions within the larger online group, a smaller group chat of five people emerges, all bound by a shared commitment to fitness. Surprisingly, a strong bond quickly forms among the five of you, despite age differences that span decades. Although the constraints of busy schedules limit regular face-to-face meetings, your camaraderie thrives through daily group messages. What initially revolved around discussions related to fitness goals gradually evolves into something deeper—a profound connection that encompasses all aspects of your lives. Within this digital realm, you openly share everything from workout achievements to personal challenges, mundane daily activities, and even moments of silliness and laughter, nurturing a unique sense of trust and companionship. This online thread that weaves through your lives transforms your interactions into something unexpectedly beautiful and immensely valuable—a friendship that knows no geographical (or age) bounds, providing a support network of confidants who truly understand and stand by you.

- **Reflect:** Think about how technology plays a role in maintaining or deepening a friendship. How does digital communication bridge the gap and keep the connection strong? Consider the ways in which technology has enabled you to connect with friends who are geographically distant. How has this digital closeness affected your sense of companionship and support? Think about the various forms of digital communication you use to stay in touch with friends, such as texting, social media, video calls, and online communities. What unique benefits does technology bring to the table?

In this chapter, we emphasized a foundational tenet of strong friendships—communication. Even amid life's hustle, we must prioritize connecting with friends. The hectic nature of our daily routines should not fracture these relationships; rather, communication should serve to preserve them. Communication comes in many forms, and, no matter the method we choose to express our thoughts and feelings, it is the authenticity and openness in our approach that foster deeper connections.

Our modern, digitally-driven society offers countless ways to keep in touch, to show sincere interest and care, and to convey love and appreciation. While we often rely on digital means to stay connected, we must not overlook the unique depth that face-to-face conversations and the human touch bring to our relationships, always mindful of personal comfort zones. The vulnerability inherent in open, honest communication may seem intimidating, but it is precisely this openness that cultivates courage and deepens our connections. By committing to and practicing real dialogue and transparency, we can significantly enrich our friendships.

CHAPTER FOUR

Accepting

Friendship quality is directly linked to empathy, the ability to resonate with others' emotions, understand their thoughts and feelings, and act accordingly.[1] *Research, in fact, shows that in stressful times, people turn to a select few friends for support, valuing most those who demonstrate empathy.*[2]

In this chapter, we turn our attention to another vital aspect of friendships: Accepting. This isn't just about tolerating quirks or managing occasional letdowns. It means wholeheartedly embracing our friends in all their complexity, valuing their unique identities, nurturing open communication, and offering steadfast support as they grow and change. Acceptance in friendship is reciprocal; as we seek understanding, we must also grant it. The depth of a friendship is closely linked to empathy—the ability to truly feel another's emotions, comprehend their perspectives, and respond with understanding.[3] Yet, acceptance isn't always straightforward, especially when we're faced with differences that challenge our own beliefs. A point worth underscoring: During trying times, most people lean on a handful of close friends, especially valuing those who exude genuine empathy and acceptance.[2] By the end of this chapter, you will gain practical tools and insights to enhance your understanding and displays of acceptance, laying the groundwork for even richer and more fulfilling friendships.

1. **Accept disappointment with grace.** Just like other important people in our lives, friends occasionally let us down. In the grand scheme of life, these disappointments often are minor (things like running late for a get-together, not responding to messages promptly, forgetting an occasion, or canceling plans). You don't have to totally dismiss these minor letdowns, but it's equally important not to excessively dwell on them. In the context of disappointment, grace involves showing understanding, empathy, or kindness toward someone who has made a mistake or transgression without necessarily requiring them to apologize. It often implies giving someone the benefit of the doubt or choosing not to hold their actions against them, even if they haven't explicitly asked for forgiveness. Grace is an attitude and a practice of releasing negative feelings or resentment. Open communication is vital for addressing and resolving friendship issues, but there are times, particularly in response to minor transgressions or disappointments, when choosing to release these feelings without explicit discussion is best. While extending grace in these moments may depend on our values and the nature of the friendship, grace always remains an available option to us and a personal choice to respond with understanding and empathy. Embracing disappointment with grace allows us to navigate these everyday imperfections, while maintaining a balanced perspective on friendships. A true test of our capacity for forgiveness comes during more significant breaches of trust or deeper hurt (more on this in number three below).

- **Envision:** The excitement had been building for weeks as you and your friend looked forward to the live jazz concert downtown, a rare chance to see a favorite artist perform. But just days before the concert, your friend calls, their voice filled with tension, "I can't believe I let this slip, but I promised another friend to help with their new apartment move this weekend, and I am the only help they have." The weight of your shared anticipation makes the news harder to take, and you can't hide your disappointment. However, recognizing the sincerity in their apology and the tough spot they're in, you choose to let go of any frustration. "We'll catch another show soon, no worries," you reassure them, genuinely meaning it. It's these moments of understanding and flexibility that not only preserve but also deepen the trust and appreciation between you. By offering them grace, your bond becomes even stronger through this little hiccup.

- **Reflect:** Pause to reflect on your expectations of your friends. Are your expectations realistic, or do they lean toward perfection? Consider instances when a friend disappointed you in the past and how you responded to those situations. How can you adjust your expectations to foster a more understanding and compassionate approach to your friendships? Embracing disappointment with grace leads to healthier and more authentic connections with those we hold dear.

2. **Find a way through hurt feelings.** Let's be honest—friendship hurt is a distinct and piercing kind of pain. When it stems from a breach of trust or a serious letdown, it cuts deeper than everyday disappointments. Such emotional wounds, often compounded by anger,

require careful navigation toward healing. Open communication with the friend who has caused you pain is crucial; it's the first step in understanding the underlying issues and beginning the delicate process of rebuilding trust. While it's perfectly acceptable to take a pause on interactions to collect your thoughts and emotions, be mindful not to let a brief hiatus extend indefinitely. Days can easily slip into weeks, then months or years, if intense feelings are left unaddressed, potentially eroding the foundations of a friendship you hold dear. That said, people sometimes find it challenging to openly communicate their extreme disappointment, pain, or anger, stemming from something a friend said, did, or didn't do. This creates an invisible barrier within your relationships. Addressing these deeper hurt feelings is paramount to preventing them from festering and souring your bonds or—sometimes worse—keeping you in the exhausting and stagnant place of mixed emotions. Though discussing such emotions can be daunting due to the vulnerability we feel and our fear of potential conflict or rejection, it's essential. Embracing open and honest dialogue is the path to bridge emotional gaps and strengthen connections, especially when anger and hurt go hand in hand. While grace is valuable, these situations usually require more than grace alone. Resolving profoundly hurt feelings may take time, but it's a necessary step toward mutual healing.

- **Envision:** You're having brunch at a restaurant with a group of friends. You jokingly bring up an old story from college days about a time when your friend made a public speaking gaffe during a class presentation, thinking it would be a light-hearted trip down memory lane. Back in the day, it was a running joke among your circle due to the nature of the mistake. As laughter fills the table, you glance over to see your friend's face clouded with discomfort. It quickly dawns on you that the story, which might have been amusing to others, was a sensitive memory for your friend. You can't help but notice the change in their demeanor. Their usual warmth is replaced by a palpable distance. You pull them aside privately and ask, "Is everything okay?" After a short pause, they admit, "Your comment hurt. I believe you didn't mean to, but it struck a chord with a sensitive issue I'm grappling with now." Unknown to you, your friend recently faced rejection following a job interview filled with blunders for a job they very much wanted. The story you told brought back the feelings of embarrassment from that college experience. Instead of getting defensive, you genuinely listen, validate their feelings, and offer a thoughtful apology. You both agree to touch base later in the week. This exchange, steeped in honesty and empathy, not only mends the rift but deepens the understanding between you two.

- **Reflect:** Think back to times when you sensed unspoken pain in a friend that you possibly caused. How did these moments shape your friendship bond? Have there been times when you struggled to share your feelings? Consider the hurdles that sometimes stand in the way of open discussions and resolutions. What fears or reservations might be at play? On the flip side, imagine the potential growth and understanding that can arise from confronting these silent wounds directly. How can you assure a space where friends feel at ease talking about uncomfortable emotions stemming from your interactions? How can you grow more at ease in sharing your own feelings? Reflect on the power of vulnerability and compassion in forging deeper ties with others.

3. **Forgive and let go.** In the dance of human relationships, missteps are bound to occur. However, one of the most profound gestures of acceptance in any relationship is the act of forgiveness and moving forward. A bit different from grace, forgiveness is a deliberate act of letting go of negative emotions, such as resentment, anger, or the desire for retribution, in response to someone's transgression or mistake. This process typically involves two friends mutually recognizing the wrongdoing, acknowledging the discomfort it caused, and choosing to release the negative emotions associated with it. With a goal of healing and reconciliation, forgiveness often requires open dialogue, be it through an apology or a heart-to-heart conversation. In embracing forgiveness, we free ourselves from the chains of negativity and accept the imperfections that come with our shared humanity. Acceptance doesn't mean condoning hurtful actions; it is about understanding that to err is part of being human. Clinging to resentment and refusing to forgive ultimately harms you more than anyone else. Over time, grudges can accumulate, stealing precious moments and experiences from your life. Furthermore, nursing grudges can infuse your spirit with bitterness, leading to numerous adverse effects on both your physical and mental well-being. A resilient friendship often thrives not solely on the good times but also on the forgiveness offered during less-than-ideal moments. By choosing to forgive, we acknowledge the flawed nature of our friends and ourselves. This acceptance is the soil in which the

roots of a resilient friendship grow, nourished by understanding and compassion.

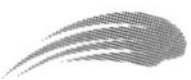

- **Envision:** For years, a delicately crafted vase passed down from your deceased grandmother has held a special place in your living room and your heart. Its intricate design is a daily reminder of the bond you shared with her. One day, as your friend is visiting, they accidentally knock over the vase. The shattering sound echoes the loss of countless stories it held. Time seems to freeze. Unfortunately, this is not the first time your friend, known for their occasional clumsiness and grand hand gestures, has damaged a cherished belonging. You feel both anger and sadness rising up. You also see the horror and regret instantly form on your friend's face. They frantically apologize, their voice trembling with guilt. Taking a deep breath, yielding to anger, you say, "Accidents happen. I know you didn't mean it. Give me a moment to sort through my emotions, then I will explain to you why this is so upsetting to me." They offer to help find a craftsman to repair it or even replace it. While the vase will never be the same, your act of understanding and forgiveness strengthens your bond, proving that the relationship holds more value than any object.

- **Reflect:** Take a moment to look inward. How do you usually react when a friend misses the mark? Are there any past grudges or grievances that still loom large in your heart? Reflect on the profound freedom and peace that forgiveness can bring into your own spirit and the rejuvenation it can bring to your friendships. Going forward, think about how you can bring more understanding into situations and release any deep-seated resentments. True friendship thrives not in the absence of faults but in the presence of abundant forgiveness.

4. **Own up to mistakes.** Remember none of us are flawless, and, just like our friends may let us down, it's also important to acknowledge our own imperfections. Whether it's forgetting a birthday, missing an important event, or unintentionally saying something hurtful, mistakes are an inevitable part of any relationship. While some friends may extend grace or readily forgive, others might require more time to process their feelings and regain trust. Regardless of the outcome, owning up to our actions, offering a sincere apology, and making amends whenever possible significantly contributes to the growth and resilience of our friendships.

- **Envision:** Your friend's child recently graduated from high school. Scrolling through social media, you see your friend's posts excitedly sharing photos of the graduation ceremony and celebrations. As your friend thanks others for their gifts and well-wishes, the realization hits: You forgot. A sharp pang of guilt settles in your chest. They've always celebrated your milestones, and here you are, having overlooked their child's graduation.

Amid the chaos of your own schedule, the announcement and date slipped your mind. Pushing aside the urge to make excuses, you call your friend. Your voice filled with regret, you confess, "I'm genuinely sorry I missed acknowledging your child's graduation. I can't believe I let this milestone event slip, and I feel terrible. It was an honest oversight, and I deeply regret not being a part of this special occasion." Showing you grace, your friend replies: "It's absolutely okay, I know how hectic life can get. Your call means a lot to us, and it really shows how much you care. Let's get together soon to celebrate in person!" You promptly send a thoughtful gift and a handwritten note to the graduate. Your friend, while initially disappointed, values your transparency and the effort you put into mending the oversight. Your genuine apology and the subsequent gesture reiterate the depth of your care and regard for their family's milestones.

- **Reflect:** Consider a time when your actions inadvertently hurt or disappointed a friend. What steps did you take to make things right? Reflect on the impact that acknowledging your mistake and seeking forgiveness had on both you and your friend. Did it change the way you interact in your friendships now? How can owning up to our mistakes influence the dynamics of a friendship? Think back to an incident where a sincere apology was needed. How did you offer that apology, and what was the response? Think about the healing process that followed—both for you and your friend. What might you do differently if faced with a similar situation in the future?

5. **Acknowledge loneliness.** Loneliness is the uncomfortable feeling people experience when they think their social life isn't as full or as meaningful as they want it to be.[4] It happens when we perceive that we don't have enough friends or when the ones we have aren't really connecting with us in a deep way.[4] Accepting loneliness means recognizing that it's a normal part of life sometimes, regardless of the number of friends you have. Lonely times happen, and they're more common than most of us care to admit. The reality is that even if you have a lot of friends and a bustling social life, there will be times when you inexplicably and painfully feel alone. And yes, it's possible to feel lonely even when you are not physically alone. Many people shy away from admitting their loneliness, thinking it reveals a personal shortcoming or weakness. However, confronting this emotion strips away its power and propels you from inertia to action. Because loneliness often stems from emotional disconnection or the lack of depth in personal interactions, reaching out to a friend—be it a close friend or an acquaintance—is especially important. Sharing your feelings with someone, even someone outside your usual friend circle, can provide you with much-needed comfort and support to help you navigate through these challenging times, reminding you that you're not alone in feeling alone.

- **Envision:** Recall a Friday night when most friends in your circle seem occupied with their own plans. You find yourself at home, overwhelmed with boredom at the thought of watching another TV series, the hours stretching ahead filling you with a sense of emptiness.

In this moment, loneliness knocks on your door. Instead of letting it take over, you decide to take action. You send a text to a neighbor you recently befriended: "Hey, it's one of those nights when the quiet feels a bit too loud. Would you be up for grabbing some dinner and catching up?" Their reply comes quick and friendly, proposing a casual restaurant just around the corner. This impromptu dinner not only chases away the solitude but also weaves a new thread of friendship into your life.

- **Reflect:** Examine your own encounters with loneliness. Have there been instances where you felt the pang of loneliness despite having a lot of friends? What insights have you gained from these experiences? Consider the lessons loneliness has taught you. Think about the significance of seeking connection and support from friends, even companionship and understanding found beyond your immediate circles. How can you prioritize reaching out and seeking reassurance when you find yourself grappling with the weight of loneliness?

6. **Practice empathy in action.** Empathy is the art of putting yourself in another person's shoes, feeling what they feel, and seeing the world through their eyes. It's like a bridge that connects hearts and fosters a deeper sense of understanding. When you practice empathy, you open up channels of connection that allow you to genuinely comprehend your friends' emotions and experiences. Practice starts with truly listening when your friends talk, not just to their words

but to the emotions underlying their stories. Ask open-ended questions that encourage them to share more about their feelings and perspectives. Use body language to convey empathy by maintaining gentle eye contact, leaning slightly forward, or offering a comforting gesture like a pat on the back or a hug, if appropriate. Allow them time to express themselves without rushing them or making them feel like they're on a timeline. Remember that empathy is not only about what you say or do; it's the authenticity of your approach and your commitment to sharing in another's emotional journey that truly matters. This level of understanding and validation helps build trust and intimacy within a relationship.

- **Envision:** Imagine your neighbor, a friend you've come to value, appearing at your doorstep unannounced one evening. Their usually bright expression is shadowed by a hint of sorrow. Sensing their need for companionship, you welcome them inside to share a warm cup of tea. As you sit down to talk in the kitchen, their voice trembles when they share that they just received the news that they didn't pass a crucial certification exam—needed for a promotion at work—that they've been working tirelessly toward for months. Their eyes reflect a mix of frustration and sadness. Instead of jumping in with solutions or playing down their emotions, you choose empathy. You take a breath, lean in with a nod, look them in the eye, and say, "I can only imagine how hard you've worked for this. This must be really tough. I'm truly sorry. What can I do to support you right now?" Your words carry not just sympathy but an authentic understanding of their disappointment. By showing empathy, you create a safe haven where they can pour out their feelings and find solace in your support.

- **Reflect:** Focus on your own capacity for empathy. How often do you truly step into your friends' emotional shoes? When was the last time you made a conscious effort to grasp others' feelings and experiences? Contemplate the ripple effect of empathy—how it transforms conversations, deepens bonds, and enhances acceptance in your friendships. Consider ways you can nurture your own abilities to show empathy. How can you actively practice seeing the world through your friends' eyes?

7. **Embrace differences with curiosity.** If you're fortunate to have a diverse circle of friends, envision them as a vibrant tapestry, with each thread representing a different background, belief, or personality. Just like a tapestry, the beauty of your friendship circle lies in its collective diversity. Diversity brings unique perspectives and flavors to your social circle. So, don't merely let your diverse circle exist without exploration or inquiry. Embracing these differences with curiosity isn't just a noble act; it's a cornerstone of strong friendships. Instead of exclusively focusing on similarities during time spent together, seize opportunities to learn and celebrate the individual stories and experiences each friend contributes. Such appreciation not only deepens relationships but also provides a more genuine sense of unity among friends, allowing us to connect on a profound level and discover fresh perspectives together. One of the beauties of a diverse circle is the chance it

offers for mutual learning and growth, enriching our lives in ways we never imagined.

- **Envision:** During a small gathering of friends one evening, the conversation drifts to the topic of religion—a subject as sensitive as it is profound. Aware of the diverse beliefs within your circle, you see this as a chance to deepen your understanding of each other. Rather than sidestepping or avoiding the details, you embrace the opportunity for open dialogue. You turn to your friend with a genuine smile and say, "I've noticed how your faith positively shapes your life; I admire that. Would you be comfortable sharing more about it? I'm really interested in learning about different viewpoints." Your friend seems delighted to have the opportunity to share. By expressing genuine curiosity and respect, you create an environment where your friend feels valued and welcomed to discuss their beliefs. This fosters a more in-depth discussion for everyone, enriching understanding of each other's worlds.

- **Reflect:** Think about the diversity in your circle of friends. How have you previously reacted or related to differences among your friends? Do you examine or embrace these cultural or perspective differences, or are you complacent? Do you find yourself wanting to change or judge your friends because of differences? Consider the benefits of an inclusive mindset for your own self-growth. How can you more deeply explore and promote an atmosphere that values diversity and cultivates acceptance?

8. **Celebrate individuality.** In a world that often demands conformity, being a champion for a friend's individuality is a genuine gift. True friendship lies in celebrating and encouraging a friend's unique qualities. It isn't just being supportive; it's a profound act of acceptance. Friendships bloom to their fullest when we cheer on our friends' unique pursuits and dreams. Our friends' passions and dreams might look different from our own, and that's all right. In fact, it's this uniqueness that makes our friendships dynamic and full of vibrancy. Supporting our friends' individual paths gives them a sense of acceptance and belonging, creating a safe space for them to explore and grow. By acknowledging and encouraging our friends' distinct qualities and ambitions, we not only enrich our friendships but also contribute to a world that values diversity and personal expression.

- **Envision:** Your longtime friend has been passionately scribbling short stories and poems in notebooks since the days of grade school. Over the years, that gleam in their eyes is unmistakable whenever they talk about a new character or plot they've conceived. Then, one day, they confide in you about their dream to become a full-time novelist. Although your career is firmly planted in the analytical world of finance, a realm far removed from the creative art of novel writing, their dream becomes something you champion as fervently as your own goals. The day they hold their first book signing, you're there in the crowd, a proud smile on your face as you wave around copies of their debut novel. Your encouragement goes beyond mere words—it's a testament to recognizing their talent and understanding the profound impact of their stories. In supporting them, you communicate, "I see and celebrate the distinct beauty and brilliance that is you."

- **Reflect:** Think about how you advocate for your friends' individual journeys. Can you recall moments where you were the cheerleader on the sidelines of their dreams? How does it feel to know you're creating a space where friends can be unabashedly themselves, without any pretense? How can you cultivate an environment that doesn't just accept but actively celebrates the diverse dreams and passions in your circle? Remember, every time you cheer on a friend's dream, you're telling them that their individuality isn't just okay—it's magnificent.

9. **Keep talking openly (even when it's hard).** It's worth repeating that in the intricate dynamics of friendship, open communication is the bedrock of trust and mutual understanding. Commit to sincere and candid discussions, even when they push you out of your comfort zone. That twinge of unease you occasionally feel about having a conversation? Often, that sense of unease is an indicator that it is time for airing out concerns. Genuine acceptance is rooted in our ability to hear and find worth in the range of emotions and perspectives of

our friends. It's not merely about expressing our own views, but about creating a sanctuary where everyone feels free to share their authentic emotions without fear of judgment or criticism. By modeling and advocating for friendships where voices aren't just heard but deeply valued and accepted, you are taking steps to ensure the longevity and depth of your bonds.

- **Envision:** Imagine that you and your friend work in the same company. Recently, your friend received a promotion to a position both of you had earnestly aspired to. You notice they're a bit hesitant to share the news with you, possibly fearing how you might react. When they finally muster the courage to tell you, you're initially hit with a pang of envy. Valuing open and honest communication, you decide to address your feelings directly. Sharing happy hour at a local pub one day after work, you say to them, "I won't lie, I felt a twinge of envy when I heard about your promotion, but that doesn't overshadow how genuinely happy I am for you. Your dedication and long hours truly paid off. I appreciate you being open with me, and I'm here to support you all the way." Your friend, visibly relieved, replies, "I was worried about how you'd take the news, and I'm so grateful for how understanding you've been. This conversation just reminds me of the strength of our friendship."

- **Reflect:** Think about how you speak with your friends. Are you truly open to what they have to say, even when the conversations are tough? Do you provide a space where they feel comfortable sharing their genuine feelings, especially during challenging moments? Reflect on the importance of active listening and affirmation in nurturing trust and fostering vulnerability. How can you adjust your communication approach to not only listen but also accept diverse emotions and viewpoints, particularly when dialogue is difficult? Remember that confronting discomfort head-on through open conversation can strengthen bonds. Embracing these differences and showing acceptance is foundational in genuine friendships, where honest, even tough, conversations serve as the cornerstone, and words act as powerful connectors.

10. **Grow together.** Relationships, like the people in them, are dynamic and ever-evolving. As individuals, our passions shift, our goals realign, and our perspectives mature. It's essential to welcome, not fear, changes in ourselves and our friends, and to celebrate the growth they represent. In the midst of these transformations, the true test of friendship is not only in acknowledging these changes but in embracing and championing them. When you actively support your friend's new endeavors or seek to understand their evolving viewpoints, you communicate a profound message: The core of your bond lies not merely in shared history but in a profound mutual respect and admiration that transcends time and change.

- **Envision:** Picture your close friend confiding in you about a bold decision that they decided to step away from a high-paying, secure job to immerse themselves in the world of watercolor painting—a passion they've long suppressed. They excitedly mention that their first show at the local library will feature a series of landscapes inspired by their recent travels. While your immediate instinct might be protective concern about the challenges and financial uncertainties that lie ahead, you opt for a path of encouragement. Recognizing the gravity of this step in their life, you pen a heartfelt note, sharing your admiration for their courage and your excitement to see their travel-inspired canvases. On the day of the exhibit at the library, you make sure to attend, beaming with pride as you view each painting. This gesture isn't merely about supporting a career shift; it's about actively honoring their journey of self-discovery.

- **Reflect:** Mull over the transformations you've observed in your friends over the years. How have you responded to their newfound interests or changes in direction? Are there times you held back your support due to your own apprehensions or biases? Ponder the depth of your acceptance when your friends unveil new chapters in their lives. How can you further elevate your role as a confidant and cheerleader during these pivotal moments? Remember, friendships that weather the storms of change are often those that shine brightest in authenticity and mutual admiration. Challenge yourself to not just be a bystander in your friend's growth journey but an active participant, encouraging and celebrating every new step they take.

11. **Concede that mutual understanding isn't a given.** Your friends won't always fully grasp your perspective or share identical viewpoints—this isn't a friendship deal-breaker, so let go of that expectation. Unless there's a significant breach of core principles, avoid allowing these differences to strain your bond. Instead, respect diverse opinions and values, even when they differ from your own. It's perfectly fine to acknowledge and embrace these differences, allowing individuality to flourish within your friendships. Savor the unique connections you share with each person, while remembering that complete agreement isn't a prerequisite for a fulfilling friendship.

- **Envision:** One of your close friends initiates a conversation about politics, and you realize that they don't fully grasp your political views, which differ from their own. Instead of getting into a heated debate or feeling frustrated, you acknowledge and respect their right to hold different beliefs and opinions. Choosing to maintain the peace and positive aspects of your friendship, you offer a gentle pivot: "I appreciate your willingness to share your perspective on these political issues, and I recognize we have different stances. But let's focus on the things that bond us. Remember our camping trip last summer? Let's plan another one. Our passion for the outdoors is just one of the many things that I value in our friendship. Let's celebrate that." By reminding both of you of the shared interests and experiences that bring joy, you underscore the importance of acceptance and mutual respect, showcasing that your friendship can thrive on common ground, despite differences in other areas."

- **Reflect:** Think about the nature of acceptance in your friendships. When friends misunderstand you or hold different views, how do you typically react? Are you able to comfortably embrace these differences, or do you find them challenging? Can you think of a time when embracing a friend's different perspective strengthened your relationship? Are there topics you tend to avoid to maintain harmony? How do you navigate these boundaries while still fostering a deep connection? Ponder the individuality that each friend brings to your life. How do these unique perspectives enrich your social circle? Consider ways you can actively show acceptance and appreciation for these differences to build a more inclusive and supportive network of friends.

12. **Be a reliable friend.** In the fabric of friendships, reliability is golden. Being a reliable friend means more than just occasional gestures of goodwill. It's a steadfast commitment to being present, both in moments of celebration and in the shadows of despair. Simply put: Show up! Your consistency, your willingness to prioritize their needs, and your attentive, empathetic presence all contribute to a nurturing environment where trust and understanding flourish. Reliability builds a foundation of trust that can weather the trials and triumphs of life, letting your friends know they can count on

you when it matters most. Understand that being reliable doesn't mean losing yourself or sacrificing your needs but rather involves weaving the threads of mutual support and understanding. Your unwavering support and dependability not only strengthen the bonds of friendship but also provide a stable pillar of comfort and security in an unpredictable world.

- **Envision:** Imagine receiving a text from a friend who's going through a rough patch in their marriage. The text carries a weight that you can feel through the screen, hinting at the gravity of their struggle. You sense the urgency and know they are seeking not just sympathy but a true connection. Despite the whirlwind of your own schedule, you quickly text back, "Let's meet up. How about a walk in the park tomorrow evening to talk it out? Just you and me." On a quiet walk the next night, your phone switched off, your attention undivided, you let them unravel their thoughts, their fears. You listen, not just with your ears but with your heart. Your responses are not filled with advice but with understanding, validation, and compassion. Your presence, devoid of judgments or expectations, becomes a balm for them. By being present, authentically and wholeheartedly, you convey that they have your support and confidence during this difficult time.

- **Reflect:** Reflect on your role as a steadfast supporter in your friends' lives. How often do you serve as a solid rock for them in times of need? Recall moments when

> you might have held back your support, perhaps due to your own challenges or fears. Think about what holds you back—be it time constraints, personal struggles, or discomfort with vulnerability. Ponder the equilibrium you maintain between nurturing your well-being and being available for friends. Consider ways to be that unwavering pillar, the gentle push when they need motivation, or the solace they seek in turmoil.

This chapter underscored how acceptance is a deep embrace of friends in their entirety—meeting them where they are now—with all of their strengths, imperfections, and quirks. Championing empathy, celebrating individuality, and committing to clear and open communication are crucial to building a foundation of true acceptance. Furthermore, by standing as a reliable presence in times of challenge, nurturing each other's growth, adapting to change, and cherishing shared experiences, you elevate friendships beyond mere existence. Robust acceptance creates a sanctuary where friends feel seen and valued, a place where laughter and solace can be shared in equal measure. Acceptance cultivates bonds that thrive, with deep, mutual respect that forms the very heart of dynamic friendship.

PART II

Social Tenets

CHAPTER FIVE

Blending

The significance of social blending for a person's health and longevity has been recognized for more than three decades. Research shows that people with a variety of social relationships not only live longer but also experience slower cognitive decline, enhanced resistance to disease, and improved outcomes with serious illnesses.[1]

Inevitably, we are all faced with the task of blending people from various parts of our lives. This chapter guides you through those challenges and highlights the advantages that come with this blending. When we discuss the concept of "blending," we're essentially talking about intentionally mixing our social circles. This involves bringing together people from various backgrounds, groups, or communities and facilitating their interactions, connections, and integration into a broader social network. Blending involves creating a harmonious fusion of different people and fostering meaningful connections between them. Let's be honest, with the demands of our busy lives, finding time to accomplish everything and spend quality time with everyone we care about can often feel like an insurmountable challenge. Blending friendships helps reduce that strain.

Blending our social circles also offers other benefits that might surprise you. Engaging a diverse array of friends can be a boost for our mental well-being, serve as a protective shield for loneliness, help our brains remain sharp as the years roll on, and enrich our understanding and acceptance of others.[2] [3] Beyond emotional and cognitive perks, blending can open doors to unexpected professional opportunities. And the cherry on top: A medley of social connections can boost our physical health.[2] As we dive deeper into the concept of blending, it's worth noting that blending isn't always easy. This chapter will help you proceed with consideration and care, ensuring that the blended interactions are positive and inclusive for everyone involved.

1. **Embrace nuanced social vibes.** Blending is an art that hinges on understanding individual quirks or preferences as much as it does on merging them. Each person in our lives brings a distinct set of traits and tendencies to our social table. Remember that not everyone will sync up seamlessly, and that's perfectly fine. The key lies in recognizing these different vibes and respecting them. Before diving headfirst into blending various circles, take a moment to grasp your friends' nuances. This understanding will guide you in figuring out which friends might effortlessly blend and where you might need to tread with a bit more caution.

- **Envision:** Picture this—you've set up a movie night at your place, inviting two friends whose enjoyment for films is as deep as yours. One friend enjoys a quiet, intimate setting for watching and discussing movies. The other delights in expressing their reactions loudly, thriving in a livelier group setting. As the night progresses, it's evident that while they both love watching movies, their viewing styles don't necessarily mesh well together. Taking this cue, instead of trying to force fit them, you opt for a different approach next time. You arrange a serene viewing experience with your quieter friend to allow for thoughtful conversation post-movie. For your more vocal friend, you organize an energetic group screening where lively banter is part of the fun. By tailoring movie nights to each friend's preferences, you create enjoyable and comfortable experiences for all, including yourself, demonstrating your thoughtful consideration of their individual personalities.

- **Reflect:** Recall moments of blending from your past, where you have given careful thought to understanding and respecting individual preferences. Were there instances when you sensed contrasting vibes between friends? How did you steer through these varied dynamics, ensuring each friend felt valued? Did you ever feel the need to make superficial compromises just for the sake of harmony? To preserve the authenticity of your relationships moving forward, how might you ensure that while blending, you're not pressing relationships into a mold they don't naturally fit into?

2. **Harmonize with your partner's social rhythms.** If you are romantically coupled, blending often feels like a dance between your social circles and those of your partner. It's important to recognize that your partner will naturally have their own distinct tastes, values, and personality that might diverge from those of your friends. Embrace the possibility that your partner might connect more with some friends than with others (and vice versa). By valuing their

individuality and creating room for them to forge their own bonds, you're nurturing a harmonious overlap between your romantic relationship and your friendships. While it is an easy trap to fall into, it's important to not neglect your friendships if you're in a committed romantic relationship. Couples often become less connected to their friends over time, but blending friendships provides strategies to navigate this challenge effectively.

- **Envision:** Let's say your partner has a deep appreciation for wine. Unlike your partner, many of your friends are passionate about sports. But, there's that one friend in your circle who, like your partner, is also more of a wine enthusiast than a sports buff. Seizing this shared interest, you plan a visit to a local winery, allowing your partner and friend to bond over their mutual passion for bold red wines. This thoughtful gesture not only helps integrate your partner into your social group but also strengthens the shared bonds among all of you. By orchestrating such interactions based on mutual interests, you create an environment where everyone feels recognized and valued for their distinctive preferences.

- **Reflect:** Think about the interplay of interests between your partner and your circle of friends. Have you noticed common passions that could be the seeds for deeper connections, or perhaps some disparities that require a thoughtful touch? Consider how these similarities and differences have shaped your social engagements. Ponder strategies to not only bridge the gaps but also to celebrate the distinct qualities each person brings to the table. Contemplate how you can craft gatherings that are harmonious and enjoyable for all involved.

3. **Cultivate couple companionship.** Being part of a couple brings its own set of joys and challenges. It can be a boon to befriend other couples who understand the dynamics of romantic partnership. These couple friendships often pave the way for collective adventures, shared wisdom, and distinct types of mutual support. Engaging with other couples not only adds richness to your social experiences but also enriches the bond you share with your partner. Sometimes, these friendships develop naturally, while other times, seeking them out might feel a bit awkward. Nevertheless, couple friendships serve as a wellspring of collective joy and shared experiences.

- **Envision:** Having recently moved to a bustling new city, you and your partner's circle of friends is still taking shape. At a laid-back neighborhood barbecue, hosted by a colleague, you click with another couple over a lively debate about the best local eateries and shared tales of travel mishaps. The chemistry is palpable. As the night winds down, you take the initiative to exchange phone numbers, seeing potential for a great friendship. The very next day, with a blend of eagerness and a touch of the jitters, you send them a message: "We had a fantastic time getting to know you both! Would you be up for joining us for dinner later this week? We'd love to continue our conversation and enjoy your company again." To your delight, they respond enthusiastically. Fast forward, these budding friendships bloom, injecting a vibrant layer of camaraderie and joy into your life and relationship.

- **Reflect:** Consider your current friendships with other couples. How have these relationships enhanced the dynamics of your own partnership? Ponder the shared laughter, collective memories, and the reciprocal support that enrich your lives. If you're new to cultivating couple friendships, consider the simple actions you could initiate. Perhaps it's sending a friendly text to connect or extending an informal invitation for dinner out or a hike. These small gestures can lay the groundwork for deeply rewarding, intertwined relationships that benefit both you and your partner.

4. **Dance delicately with family and friends.** Navigating the dynamics between friends and family members—be it parents, siblings, or adult children—can be like a dance that requires poise, timing, and a keen sensitivity to the people involved. Both of these groups hold special places in your heart, yet they often operate at distinct rhythms. While some friends may seamlessly integrate into a lively and intimate atmosphere of family interactions, reveling in the closeness and camaraderie, others might feel more like outsiders, preferring more casual settings. On the flip side, family members may occasionally prefer the familiarity of family-only get-togethers without the infusion of

new or less familiar faces. By being perceptive and responsive to everyone's comfort levels, you can create welcoming environments where people feel acknowledged, relaxed, and truly at home.

- **Envision:** Let's say you're planning a birthday celebration for yourself at home and are toying with the idea of inviting both your close friends and family members. Going through your invitation list, you realize that some of your friends might not relish a family-oriented setting or might not be too keen on wading through childhood tales with your aunts and uncles. You begin to feel some angst about blending everyone. To honor everyone's comfort zones, including your own, you opt for two distinct gatherings: one for family and another for friends. This approach lifts the internal pressure you feel and ensures that both your friends and family can celebrate in settings where they're most at ease, allowing everyone, especially you, to savor the birthday celebrations to the fullest.

- **Reflect:** Merging friends and family can offer both rewarding connections and unique challenges. Were there times in the past when blending these groups was beneficial? Or perhaps instances where it was less than ideal? Consider how these dynamics influenced your relationships and the overall atmosphere during blended gatherings. As you look ahead, what strategies can you use to ensure a sensitive and respectful approach to these intersections of your social circles?

5. **Lead through social tensions.** When different friend groups come together or new friends are introduced to your existing circle, it's natural to hope for instant connections. It's equally natural for there to be initial differences, awkwardness, or even conflicts. Instead of feeling disheartened, view these moments as rich opportunities for growth and understanding. Cultivate a mindset of patience and open-mindedness, recognizing that real friendships often take time to flourish. Give people the breathing space to connect on their own terms. Even if bonds don't form immediately, remain hopeful; friendships have a way of blossoming when least expected. Stay open, flexible, and receptive to the evolving dynamics within your social circle.

- **Envision:** You've always been close with a group of friends from your childhood days. Recently, you connected with someone from your past who just moved to your city. Eager to bring these two worlds together, you arrange a relaxed cook-out at your place. As the day approaches, excitement mingles with a touch of nerves. How will your longtime friends connect with this new addition? The evening begins with polite small talk, everyone gauging personalities and even indulging in playful banter. Rather than leaving the gathering to chance, you step into the role of an active host, steering conversations toward shared passions and encouraging open dialogue. A few hours in, you notice your childhood friends and the newcomer engaged in animated conversation over mutual interests. While the night doesn't conclude with any vows of lifelong friendship, there's a clear sense that new relationships might deepen in the future. You come to understand that blending friend groups isn't about insisting on immediate bonds but creating a space where they might naturally develop.

- **Reflect:** Think back to a time when you brought together different friend groups or introduced new friends to your existing circle. How did you feel initially about the potential for friends not getting along? Were you anxious, hopeful, or indifferent? What role did you play in the interaction—a mediator, a spectator, or an active participant? Were there any challenges or conflicts that emerged during the gathering or subsequent interactions? Did any unexpected connections form, or did the friendships remain separate? Consider how these insights can help navigate and enhance future social situations.

6. **Applaud spontaneous bonds.** Although mixing different friend groups doesn't always result in instant connections and can take time to blossom, your introductions sometimes spark unexpected chemistry between different friends. By providing an environment where authentic, organic connections can form, you pave the way for fresh friendships among others. Encourage these new connections with an open heart, free from jealousy or resentment, cherishing the role you play in expanding the circle of companionship among those you care for. Trust in the potential these bonds hold

to bring joy and fulfillment to those involved, even if you aren't at the center of them.

- **Envision:** Think about two relatively new friends—one you met volunteering at the food bank and another you met playing pickleball. You invite them both to go out to dinner. Throughout the evening, you observe that they're drawn to each other, bonding over their mutual passion for health and fitness. A few weeks later, in a casual conversation with your co-volunteer, you find out the two of them have been running together. While you were the bridge that connected them, their burgeoning friendship seems to be charting its own course. Instead of feeling left out, you're delighted. Their newfound camaraderie not only means they've discovered a shared interest, but it also augments the harmony when all three of you are together.

- **Reflect:** Look back on instances when you acted as a bridge, connecting friends who later formed their own unique bond. How did it make you feel to witness those friendships blossom? While it's natural to sometimes feel a twinge of insecurity or jealousy when two friends connect independently, remember to focus on the broader implications for your social circle. Organic connections introduce new dynamics, enriching conversations, and shared experiences. As you ponder these instances, think about your future gatherings. How can you create an environment that encourages such organic connections while also ensuring you remain an integral part of these expanding circles?

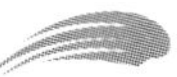

7. **Craft inclusive activities.** The magic of blending social circles is curating experiences that allow a range of personalities to connect effortlessly. When planning group activities, aim to weave together elements that cater to different tastes. This might mean merging interests, like arts and sports, or balancing relaxation with adventure. Activities like outdoor excursions, themed game nights, concerts, interactive dinners, or shared cultural experiences can bridge the gaps between varied interests. Be attentive to everyone's comfort zones, physical abilities, and any accessibility requirements. Tailor-made experiences not only encourage deeper bonds among friends but also celebrate the rich interests and backgrounds within your social network.

- **Envision:** Picture this—you have a few friends who love cooking and others who are all about board games. You decide to host an event that marries these interests, a Culinary Game Night. To set the mood and manage expectations, you send out a group text: "Hey all, super excited for our Culinary Game Night! A little something for everyone. Bring a dish that showcases your culinary flair, and let's dive into some board games afterward. Can't wait for a blend of flavors, fun, and fantastic company." The evening is a big success, offering everyone a chance to showcase their passions and to bond over shared experiences.

- **Reflect:** Look back on a time when you planned or participated in a blended group activity. How did you feel about the overall dynamics and interactions of the group? Were there moments that stood out as particularly successful or moments that felt awkward or forced? How did your choices in planning or participating in the activity impact the overall experience and the connections formed? Using these insights, consider how you can enhance the inclusivity and enjoyment of future gatherings among diverse friend groups.

8. **Keep an eye on the mix.** When you gather friends from different circles, you're creating a unique social mix that can experience shifts in dynamics. While these changes can be subtle, it's important to be attuned and responsive as a considerate host and friend. Being considerate is about showing courtesy, empathy, and concern for the welfare of others. Look out for instances where some individuals dominate conversations, unintentionally leaving others on the sidelines. Be mindful of the potential formation of cliques that exclude certain friends from interactions. If conflicts arise due to differing perspectives, gently mediate and encourage understanding. Foster inclusivity by initiating discussions that draw on shared interests and organizing collaborative activities. Remember, you don't need to oversee every detail or manage every conversation. The aim is to proactively create an atmosphere where everyone feels comfortable and part of the group.

- **Envision:** Imagine you're planning a weekend getaway to a mountain cabin with a few close friends from different circles. As you map out the trip details through email threads, you observe that a couple of enthusiastic planners are quick to suggest and decide on the cabin location and the other activities, leaving little room for others to chime in. Being mindful of the dynamics at play, you propose methods to include everyone's input, such as a round-robin email where each person proposes an idea, voting on major decisions, or a shared document that everyone can contribute to. This approach not only ensures that everyone's perspective is considered but also weaves a collaborative spirit into the heart of your adventure, ensuring the weekend reflects a collective vision, and enhances the anticipation and fun for everyone involved.

- **Reflect:** Think back to a situation when you noticed some individuals overshadowed others in a group setting. Consider the effects of this dynamic on the group's cohesion. How did such dynamics impact the overall group engagement? Were you proactive in addressing the imbalance? Reflect on your techniques to enhance inclusivity in group decision-making. Do they help provide a sense of equality and participation? Consider these experiences as valuable tools to nurture balanced dynamics.

9. **Preserve individual bonds and connections.** While blending and broadening friend groups can lead to collective bonding, remember it is the individual connections that anchor these relationships. Shared group activities can undoubtedly foster unity, camaraderie, and communal spirit, but individual relationships are foundational to group cohesion. The distinction here is that while collective experiences are valuable, they are built upon the foundation of strong individual relationships. Because the strength of a group is derived from the strength of individual bonds, be sure to maintain one-on-one connections to preserve the integrity and vibrancy of the group as a whole. By ensuring that individual friendships are consistently nurtured alongside group engagements, a harmonious blend is achieved, where both collective spirits and profound personal bonds flourish.

- **Envision:** Consider a dear friend you bonded with when you first moved into your neighborhood. Over time, as both of you expanded your families and social circles, group hangouts became more frequent than one-on-one time. One evening, while in the midst of a boisterous neighborhood block party, you lean in and say, "You know, I really value the times we all hang out together, but I miss our heart-to-heart chats. How about we revive our old tradition and grab lunch at that bistro downtown next week? Just us, like old times." Setting aside this dedicated time allows for intimate conversations and makes memories, ensuring the unique bond remains untainted amid the evolving group dynamics.

- **Reflect:** Think about the delicate balance between group dynamics and individual friendships. Consider the unique role that one-on-one relationships play in your social well-being and the different layers of support, trust, and intimacy they provide. Have you experienced moments where close friendships felt diluted within the broader context of group activities? Recall the emotions that arose from this shift and how you addressed them. How can you ensure these personal connections receive the attention they deserve, even as your social circle expands?

10. **Manage conflict.** When undercurrents of conflict ripple through your circle of friends, whether they manifest as palpable silence or covert friction between people, it's important to navigate the situation with care and diplomacy. While it's not your place to resolve their issues, you can still serve as a catalyst for harmony. Continue to engage with each friend individually, providing a listening ear without pressing for details, steering toward unsolicited advice, or pushing for reconciliation. Cultivate environments conducive to healing, like gatherings centered around shared interests that naturally diffuse tension. Be vigilant against inadvertently fueling gossip or taking sides. Your role is to be an impartial source of comfort, promoting peace and understanding in subtle ways, all while safeguarding your own peace of mind and emotional boundaries.

- **Envision:** Imagine you're a part of a close-knit group of friends, a circle where everyone has always enjoyed each other's company. However, recently you noticed a change—two of your friends stopped speaking to each other. The once harmonious atmosphere is now tinged with tension. In response, you continue to spend quality time with each friend separately, engaging in activities you've always enjoyed together. One of your friends opens up about the situation during a walk. You listen attentively, offering support without prying by saying: "I've noticed things have been a bit different lately, and while I don't need to know all the details, I want you to know that I'm here for you. We all go through rough patches, and I'm committed to being there for both of you." Rather than intervening or taking sides, you choose to be a source of stability. You convey that your role is one of understanding and patience, allowing your friends to sort through their conflict at their own pace. This considerate approach preserves your individual friendships and contributes to a sense of respect and well-being within the circle.

- **Reflect:** Consider a time when you noticed two friends within your circle having a conflict. Recall the strategies you employed to navigate this delicate situation. What insights did you gain about the role of clear, open communication in preserving group harmony? Weigh the importance of remaining impartial while offering support and implementing methods to foster resolution without compromising your neutrality. How can you facilitate an environment that encourages understanding and mutual respect, even when disagreements arise?

In summary, the act of blending friend groups is both an art and a vital element of our social well-being. As we weave together diverse sets of friends and introduce new people into our established circles, we not only broaden our social networks but also tap into the myriad benefits that rich social interactions offer for our mental and physical health. This chapter explained that while this journey of integration is intricate and sometimes challenging, we don't need to shy away from it. Through thoughtful blending—by respecting individual boundaries, orchestrating inclusive activities, attentively navigating group dynamics, and cherishing individual friendships—we can cultivate a social environment that's as vibrant as it is supportive. Indeed, blending may require finesse, but the resulting mosaic of interconnected friendships enhances our lives in immeasurable ways.

CHAPTER SIX

Safeguarding

When we trust our friends, we have confidence that we can rely on them to care about us and be responsive to our needs, now and in the future.[1] *No relationship can survive if trust is missing.*[2]

Welcome to chapter six, where we explore the profound importance of trust in the realm of safeguarding within friendships. Trust is the cornerstone of strong friendships, a solid base built on reliability, loyalty, and unwavering faith in one another. It is this foundational belief that gives us confidence our friends will care for us and be responsive to our needs, both now and in the future.

Safeguarding is a natural extension of this trust—it's about being present as a steadfast supporter and advocate for our friends, especially during challenging times. This role involves actively defending and upholding our friends' interests, offering unwavering support, and championing their causes when they cannot do so themselves. It is a characteristic often associated with altruism, reflecting our deep commitment to the well-being of those we care about. Being trusted enriches our own sense of self-worth and belonging, and it is from this place of security that we are compelled to safeguard our friends—actively protecting their interests and well-being as a true testament to our shared trust. In safeguarding the bond, we not only protect but also fortify the trust that underpins the entire fabric of our friendships.

Trusting and being trusted are crucial pillars of healthy friendships and overall well-being. Trusting a friend provides a sense of safety, allows vulnerability, and enables mutual support, fostering open communication and the sharing of emotions. This foundation of reliability and integrity reduces stress and enhances the quality of relationships. Conversely, being trusted by our friends affirms our credibility, encourages personal growth, and contributes to a positive self-image. These dynamics are pivotal for our mental and emotional health, playing a vital role in deepening and sustaining the longevity of our friendship bonds.

As you dive deeper into this chapter, you'll uncover valuable insights and practical strategies to not only cultivate trust but also stand up and safeguard your friends, building lasting and fulfilling connections that transcend the ordinary.

1. **Keep an eye on well-being and safety.** As a reliable and trusted friend, it's paramount to have your friends' best interests at heart. This involves keeping a watchful eye on their physical safety and overall wellness. Being proactive means guiding them away from risky or harmful situations. If you notice them heading into potential harm or danger, offer supportive advice and encouragement to make wiser choices. Also, avoid enabling behaviors that could put their safety at risk. While it might seem like common sense, let's face it, even adults sometimes make questionable decisions! Your role is to be a responsible and caring presence, ensuring that their protection and welfare are a priority.

- **Envision:** Imagine you're at a beach outing with friends, and despite warning flags for strong currents, one of your friends decides to swim in the risky area. Recognizing the potential danger, you approach them to express your concern about the currents and the warning flags: "Hey, I saw the warning flags on the beach. Let's play it safe and swim in a different area or play some bocce on the beach instead." Grateful for your vigilance, your friend agrees: "Good call—I hadn't spotted the flags. Let's stick to dry sand for now." This moment not only demonstrates your care and attentiveness but also underscores the importance of looking out for each other's well-being.

- **Reflect:** Recall moments when you intervened to safeguard your friends from potential harm. How did you approach the situation? What was your friend's reaction? Reflect on any times you hesitated to step in and the reasons behind that hesitation. How can you strike a balance between being protective and respecting their independence? Consider the impact of your actions on your friendships and the trust that emerges from your genuine concern for their well-being.

2. **Guide friends away from compromising situations.** A genuine friend looks out for the best interests of their companions, especially in public settings. Friendship goes beyond merely enjoying good times together; it involves ensuring that your friends don't unknowingly place themselves in circumstances that could tarnish their image,

dignity, or reputation. Your role as a caring friend extends to recognizing situations that might lead to embarrassment or harm their reputation and gently steering them away from such situations. In doing so, you're not only looking after their immediate welfare but also preserving the strength and respect of their relationships across various social circles. Being attentive and discreet in such situations showcases your commitment to a supportive, protective friendship.

- **Envision:** Imagine you're attending a small dinner party at a friend's house. Laughter and conversation fill the air as everyone enjoys good food and company. As the evening unfolds and the champagne flows, one of your close friends becomes increasingly animated while sharing stories with the group. Unfortunately, their stories take a turn into inappropriate territory, and you notice the discomfort on the faces of other guests. Sensing the need to step in, with tact and consideration, you smoothly shift the conversation to a different topic, steering away from the awkward situation. Your timely intervention not only protects your friend from potential embarrassment but also helps maintain the positive vibe of the gathering.

- **Reflect:** Recall a time when you shielded your friends from situations that potentially affected their reputation or caused embarrassment later on. How did you decide when to step in? Consider the challenges of gracefully guiding friends away from potentially embarrassing scenarios. How can you strike a balance between preserving their reputation and allowing them to have fun? Think about the trust that grows from your thoughtful actions and how they contribute to the strength of your friendship.

3. **Safeguard confidentiality: Being a trustworthy friend means honoring the privacy and secrets shared with you, creating a safe space for open and honest communication.** Respecting confidentiality is like building a vault of trust where your friends confide in you without fear. Being a trustworthy friend entails more than just keeping secrets; it requires a deep understanding of the responsibility that comes with someone else's trust. Every piece of information shared in confidence reinforces the belief that you are a reliable pillar of support. Therefore, except in critical circumstances where silence could lead to harm, the secrets entrusted to you should remain secure within the walls of your integrity. This unwavering commitment to confidentiality helps to forge stronger bonds and nurtures a truly supportive friendship. Everyone benefits from having at least one confidant!

- **Envision:** Picture a scenario where you're spending time with a close friend, someone you've shared laughter and tears with. You're walking together along a secluded trail in the local park, a place where nature has often been the backdrop for deep conversations with them. They ask to talk with you confidentially, their expression carrying a mix of anxiety and vulnerability. They reveal something deeply personal—they're grappling with the idea of ending their marriage. Their words are raw and sincere, as they share their innermost struggles, fears, and uncertainties. In that moment, you feel the weight of their trust resting on your shoulders. You realize that they've chosen to confide in you because they see you as someone they can rely on, someone who will respect their privacy and keep their thoughts safe. You say: "Thank you for trusting me with this. I can't imagine how hard it must be; I'm here for you. What you shared stays between us—your privacy is my utmost priority. How can I support you further?" As you listen, you're reminded of the profound bond you share and the responsibility that comes with being their confidant. It's a reminder that trust is not just a word—it's a commitment to be there for your friend, to hold their trust close, and to provide the unwavering support they need.

- **Reflect:** Think about the significance of keeping secrets between friends. How does respecting confidentiality contribute to building trust? Consider instances where you were entrusted with sensitive information and the impact it had on your friendship. Recall how you felt if there was a time when you didn't honor a friend's confidentiality or when someone didn't honor yours. How can you ensure that you are a reliable secret keeper? Explore the emotional responsibility that comes with being a confidant and how it strengthens the bond you share with your friends.

4. **Steer clear of gossip and rumors.** Gossip, which involves sharing sensational or private information about someone without their consent, is a betrayal of trust. Gossiping about a friend can slowly erode a strong foundation of trust and seriously harm the connection you share. As a genuine and reliable friend, resist the temptation to spread rumors or share private information about your friends. Just don't do it. Instead, if you're privy to sensitive information, choose to be a pillar of support, a confidante who helps keep the integrity of friends' personal stories intact. This type of disciplined discretion strengthens the bonds of friendship and builds an environment where everyone feels secure in sharing their life with you. Engaging in gossip about others sets a precedent that may lead friends to rightfully suspect you do the same about them. Cultivate an atmosphere of integrity by ensuring your friends never have to wonder about your discretion; your steadfast respect for their privacy will affirm the trust they place in you.

- **Envision:** Imagine you're casually chatting with friends on a Saturday morning, all of you gathered around the edge of the soccer field, eyes on your children's match. The discussion takes a turn toward a rumor involving someone within your friend circle. In that moment, you feel the temptation to contribute your own thoughts or pieces of information to the discussion. But, you quickly catch yourself and remember the negative consequences of gossip. You shift the focus by saying "Has anyone tried that new restaurant in town? I've heard great things and was thinking of checking it out for lunch after the match. Is anyone interested?" This tactful change of subject not only diverts attention from the rumor but also sends a clear message of your disengagement from the gossip. Instead, you set an example of a healthy and positive exchange. By carefully choosing your words and refraining from spreading rumors, you uphold your commitment to being a trustworthy friend.

- **Reflect:** Mull over a time when you successfully refrained from engaging in or contributing to gossip. What strategies did you use to redirect yourself? How did you feel afterward? Were there times you didn't refrain? Consider the impact of your actions on the overall trust within your group of friends. Have you ever been the subject of gossip? How did you feel? What steps can you take to cultivate positive habits that contribute to a more respectful and positive friendship circle, free from gossip?

5. **Defend against disparaging remarks or actions.** Being a true friend means being a defender, too. Your role extends beyond just protecting your friends from external criticism—it also involves standing up for them when they succumb to self-criticism or doubt their own worth. When a friend faces unjust treatment, battles insecurities, or is subjected to disparaging remarks, your steadfast support is crucial. Confronting negativity, regardless of its source—whether from others or from within your friend—reinforces your

commitment to their well-being and solidifies the trust at the heart of your friendship.

- **Envision:** You and your friend are about to walk in the door of a highly anticipated social event at a new art gallery. As you pause outside the entrance, your friend turns to you and says, "I'm not sure if I'm dressed right for this. I hate the way I look. Everyone else is going to look so stylish." You notice the self-doubt in their voice. With a warm smile, you respond, "You know what? Your unique sense of style is one of the things I love about you. I have a feeling that your outfit will turn heads in the best possible way. Plus, I'm right here by your side. Let's go have some fun!" Your encouraging words ease their nervousness, boost their confidence, and reassure them that they belong, just as they are.

- **Reflect:** Think back to a time when you stood up for a friend who was facing criticism from others or expressing self-deprecating words. How did it feel to step in and advocate for their well-being? Were there any obstacles in addressing their negative mindset or comments? Consider the ways in which your actions influenced your friend's self-assurance and the dynamics of your friendship. Remember, your intervention not only curtails negativity but also communicates your unwavering loyalty and defense of your friend.

6. **Display empathy and understanding.** As a loyal and trusted friend, one of the primary qualities you bring to your relationships is empathy—an ability to truly understand and resonate with your friends' experiences, emotions, and challenges. Showing empathy means being a compassionate listener who offers unwavering support and validates their feelings. Keep in mind that empathy goes beyond sympathy. It involves a deeper emotional connection. While sympathy is feeling sorry for someone or acknowledging their emotions, empathy takes it a step further. When you're empathetic, you not only understand what someone is going through but you also share in their emotional experience. Intentional acts of empathy strengthen the foundation of trust and lead to a more resilient bond between friends, cultivating an environment of safety and care.

- **Envision:** One Saturday morning while walking your dogs together, your friend opens up to you about their high levels of work-related stress, including a very toxic boss. They share how overwhelmed and drained they've been feeling due to the increasing demands at their job and lack of recognition by their boss. Instead of brushing it off or offering quick solutions, you pause the walk for a moment, maintain eye contact, and say, "I'm really sorry to hear that you're going through this. It sounds like you're dealing with a lot right now. I've dealt with bad bosses so I can relate to the stress it brings. It can color your whole life." You continue, "Please know that I'm here for you, ready to listen, whenever you need to vent." Your genuine concern and willingness to acknowledge their emotions create a safe space for them to share, showing that you truly care about their well-being and are willing to provide the support they need.

- **Reflect:** Reflect on the role of empathy in your friendships. How do you demonstrate empathy toward your friends' experiences and emotions? Consider the impact of active listening, validation, and offering support in deepening your connection. How do you let people know you are truly listening? How can you better cultivate empathy in your interactions and create a space where your friends feel heard and understood?

7. **Be true to your word.** A key aspect of building trust is being trustworthy. Being true to your promises and commitments is more than just making lofty declarations. It means taking responsibility for your words and actions—and ensuring that you follow through with what you said you would do. This may involve showing up to support your friend at an important event or simply keeping your word on smaller matters, like meeting up for a hike or completing a favor. When you consistently keep your promises and commitments, your friends will develop a sense of trust in your reliability and dependability, deepening your connection and sense of mutual support. Of note—no one is perfect, and there may be times when unforeseen circumstances prevent you from fulfilling a commitment. When this happens, communicate openly and honestly with your friends, expressing your regrets and working together to find a solution. Being transparent about any changes or challenges shows

that you value their trust and are committed to open and respectful communication.

- **Envision:** Let's say you and your friend are planning a weekend getaway to a seaside cottage for their birthday. You've both been looking forward to this trip for weeks, and you promised to take care of all the logistics and preparations. As the date gets closer, you make sure everything is set, from packing essentials to providing the transportation. On the day of the trip, you pick up your friend with a big smile, excited for the adventure ahead. Throughout the weekend, you stay true to your word, ensuring that all the plans go smoothly and that your friend has a fantastic time. Your friend turns to you at one point and says, "I can't believe how well you've organized everything. It's been such a stress-free trip thanks to you. What an incredible birthday present!" In that moment, you realize that your commitment to your promises has not only deepened your friendship but also allowed you to create lasting memories together.

- **Reflect:** Think about instances when you joyfully followed through on your commitments to your friends. How did those experiences contribute to the trust between you? Consider the impact of your reliability on their perception of you as a friend. Reflect on the times when you faced challenges keeping your word and how you overcame them. How can you continue to prioritize reliability to strengthen the bonds of trust in your friendships?

8. **Share constructive criticism with kindness.** As a trusted friend, there may be times when you find yourself in situations where you need to provide honest feedback or critique to support your friend's personal growth. Sidestepping situations that require honest conversations does not do friends any favors. Handling such conversations with gentleness, empathy, and an authentic intention to help them improve is pivotal. Striking a balance between candor and tactfulness guarantees that your friend recognizes and values your motives, cultivating a deeper trust within your friendship. It's essential to deliver honest, constructive criticism in a way that is sensitive to your friend's feelings, ensuring that the feedback is perceived not as an attack but as an act of caring. Always wrap your words with encouragement, showing that you believe in their capacity to grow and that your ultimate goal is to see them thrive.

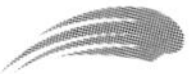

- **Envision:** Visualize that your work friend asks for your feedback on a company presentation they gave to a large audience, where you were in attendance. Meeting privately in their office, you approach the situation with care and sensitivity, acknowledging their strengths and what they did well during the presentation. You also provide constructive criticism by highlighting areas where they can enhance their delivery and organization, saying "I want to start by saying that your presentation was really engaging and had a clear flow. Your confidence while speaking definitely captured the audience's attention—and mine—and you explained complex concepts in simple terms. To make it even better next time, slow your pace down a bit. Try using more visual aids to reinforce your points and keep the audience even more engaged. You're already doing a great job, and I believe these adjustments could make your presentations even more powerful." With this approach, your feedback is specific, actionable, and focused on their professional growth.

- **Reflect:** Consider your approach to offering constructive criticism to your friends. How do you ensure that your feedback is helpful and supportive? Consider the importance of balancing positive feedback with areas for improvement. How can you provide specific and actionable suggestions that will assist your friends in their personal or professional growth? Additionally, reflect on your own receptiveness to constructive criticism and how you can create an open and safe environment where feedback is valued and embraced among friends.

9. **Actively support goals and dreams.** Another way that trust in a friendship manifests is through the active support of each other's goals and ambitions. It's about being a constant in their corner, where your support is as steadfast as it is enthusiastic. Pay attention to how you actively champion your friends' aspirations. Show your loyalty and commitment by not only cheering from the sidelines but

also stepping into their world. Engage fully in their pursuits, not just with words but through involvement. Celebrate their achievements and offer encouragement during setbacks. Encourage them to persevere in the face of obstacles, reminding them of their strengths and the progress they've made. Your unwavering belief in their potential can be a powerful catalyst, inspiring them to continue striving toward their aspirations with confidence and determination. In this journey together, your presence becomes a testament to a trust that is both felt and deeply relied upon in their pursuit of happiness.

- **Envision:** Picture your friend excitedly sharing their dream of publishing a novel. As they outline their path to publication, you engage actively, asking pointed questions about their characters and plot twists. You offer to be a beta reader, providing constructive feedback and suggestions on drafts. When they receive rejection letters from publishers, you're there to offer encouragement and remind them of famous authors who faced similar challenges. Then, the day comes when they finally hold their published book in their hands. You're at their book launch event, celebrating their achievement and proudly holding a copy of their book. You feel a sense of pride knowing that your unwavering support and collaborative spirit played a significant role in making their dream a reality.

- **Reflect:** Take a moment to think about a recent situation where a friend shared an aspiration or dream with you.

Ask yourself, how did you show that you're truly committed to their success and happiness? Reflect on the value you add when celebrating friends' victories, offering encouragement during tough times, and providing help when needed. Can you think of new ways to strengthen your position as a main encourager and partner in your friends' dreams?

10. **Practice forgiveness and resolve.** Friendships are not immune to conflicts and misunderstandings, even among the best of friends. Though we've touched on the personal consequences of holding grudges, the focus here is on repairing the friendship after a conflict has occurred. As we navigate the complexities of human emotions and interactions, forgiveness becomes a testament to the trust we place in our friendships. Trust is rebuilt and strengthened not by ignoring the issues, but through confronting them head-on with a willingness to understand and a commitment to move forward together. Addressing disagreements openly and honestly is critical to preventing conflicts from festering. Engaging in constructive dialogue, addressing conflicts openly and honestly, seeking to understand each other's perspectives, and working together to find solutions can strengthen trust and lead to deeper connections within the friendship. This process of joint problem-solving fosters a deeper level of trust, as each act of forgiveness is a building block in the foundation of a lasting friendship. Forgiveness is intertwined with trust, each reinforcing the other, creating a robust bond that can withstand the tests of time and conflict.

- **Envision:** Think about a close friend whom you've known for years. Recently, during a long text thread, a disagreement erupts between the two of you over a sensitive topic. The back and forth texting escalates into an argument, and both of you feel hurt and misunderstood. Instead of allowing the conflict to strain your friendship, you recognize the importance of addressing it. You reach out to your friend and suggest meeting to discuss the issue. "Hey, I really value our friendship and the history we share. I want you to know that I didn't intend for our disagreement to escalate like it did. I think we both got caught up in the heat of the moment, and it hurt both of us. We will get through this!" During the meeting, both of you express your perspectives and feelings, taking turns to actively listen to each other without interruption. As the discussion progresses, you both admit to being under high levels of stress, which likely contributed to the intensity of the disagreement. This understanding allows you to empathize with each other's experiences and see the situation from a different perspective. Recognizing the importance of your friendship and the shared history, you choose to let go of resentments and prioritize understanding and forgiveness. You acknowledge the impact of the disagreement on both of you and find a resolution that honors your friendship.

- **Reflect:** Consider the challenges of resolving conflicts and practicing forgiveness within your friendships. How do you typically approach disagreements and misunderstandings? What happened during the times when you let your anger and hurt linger? Consider strategies for effective communication, such as active listening and empathy. Reflect on ways to foster a culture of forgiveness and growth within your friendships. How can you create an environment that encourages open dialogue, mutual understanding, and the resolution of conflicts?

11. **Honor boundaries and personal space.** Safeguarding your friends extends to respecting their boundaries and personal space. Each person has their own unique needs for privacy, alone time, and personal boundaries. Respecting these boundaries not only shows that you value their individuality and autonomy within the friendship but also that you trust their decisions about their own well-being. Taking it a step further, respecting boundaries also involves defending or advocating for them. It means recognizing situations where their boundaries may be crossed and stepping in to address those situations. By actively defending their boundaries, you reinforce the message that their well-being and comfort are important to you. Your friends feel safe and understood, knowing that rather than judge, you respect and defend their needs and boundaries.

- **Envision:** A close friend is experiencing a health scare in their life, and they express a desire for emotional and physical space and privacy. When you check in on them, they tell you that they are not ready to discuss the details of their situation right now. In response, you honor their boundaries by refraining from prying or pressuring them for information. "Of course, I completely understand. Your well-being is important to me, and I want to support you in the way that's best for you. Whenever you're ready to talk, I'm here to listen and offer my support. In the meantime, if there's anything you need or if you change your mind, don't hesitate to reach out." By respecting their boundaries and refraining from pushing them beyond their comfort zone, you demonstrate your trust in their judgment of their own well-being.

- **Reflect:** Recall situations in which you respected the boundaries and personal space of your friends. How has this contributed to building trust and maintaining healthy friendships? Conversely, consider instances where you unintentionally crossed those boundaries, pushing too hard. How can you become more mindful and proactive in respecting the personal space of your friends? Reflect on ways to assure an environment of trust, understanding, and respect for personal boundaries in your friendships.

This chapter explored the vital aspects of building trust with friends, from ensuring their well-being to countering negativity, showing empathy, keeping promises, providing constructive feedback, backing their aspirations, resolving conflicts, and respecting boundaries. Embracing these principles fosters relationships where authenticity, support, and mutual respect flourish, leading to deeper and more rewarding connections. Trust forms the foundation of our friendships, while our commitment to safeguarding our friends demonstrates the depth of our concern. Through the active practice of trust and unwavering advocacy for our friends, we not only cultivate and fortify the bonds of friendship but also create resilient connections that provide comfort and strength against life's adversities. The rewards of trusting and being trusted extend deeply into our lives, fostering a rich sense of community and personal well-being. [3]

CHAPTER SEVEN

Reciprocating

When people believe their friends to be as generous and positive in spirit as themselves, they tend to work harder to sustain and strengthen the bond they share, offering more support and revealing more about themselves than they might otherwise. [1]

Friendships are like a beautiful dance, and at the heart of this dance is the art of giving and receiving. While we touched on aspects of this concept in previous chapters, it's here that we dive deeper into the finer moves of extending kindness and compassion to our friends, while also gracefully accepting the same. At its core, this dance is not just about the actions we take but the spirit in which we perform them, embracing each gesture of respect, empathy, and understanding as sacred. This chapter shines a light on the give-and-take that forms the heartbeat of friendship, where goodwill and support flow freely in both directions.

Reciprocity enhances the quality of our friendships because it provides an environment where positive emotions are amplified. When we give and receive with a spirit of positivity, we create a cycle of goodwill that enhances our bonds. Here's an important takeaway: Positivity in our friendships is a strong predictor of our overall sense of happiness and fulfillment.[2][3] In fact, positivity is sometimes referred to as a "seventh sense."[2] Just like our other senses help us understand and navigate the world around us, this seventh sense helps us understand how to make our friendships more fulfilling by focusing on positive aspects. It's like having a special skill for helping people feel happy when they're around us. The belief in the generosity and positivity of our friends compels us to invest more deeply in these relationships. We give more, share more, and in doing so, we reinforce the ties that bind us. Let's explore ways to strengthen positive reciprocity.

1. **Exchange time generously.** Time is a precious gift we give to our friends, so prioritize quality time with them. In the hustle and bustle of our busy lives, it's easy to get caught up in the demands of work, family, and other responsibilities, inadvertently putting our friendships on the back burner. By offering your time and attention, you are giving a part of yourself to your friends. Similarly, when you receive their time and attention, you're being gifted with moments that enrich your life, reflecting the mutual appreciation and value in your friendship. It's just about impossible to nurture quality friendships without both dedicating time to them and being open to receiving the same effort in return.

- **Envision:** Imagine a scenario where you and a close friend are caught up in your demanding jobs and personal commitments. You both realize that it's been months since you truly connected. In light of this realization, you plan a Sunday afternoon picnic at a local park. This act of planning and making time for each other shows a mutual act of intention to spend quality time together. As you enjoy the calm of the outdoors, engage in lighthearted conversations, and share the delicious food your friend prepared, the significance of time spent together becomes palpable. The experience serves as a reminder that these shared moments are invaluable for strengthening the bonds of your friendship.

- **Reflect:** Pause to consider your current approach to spending quality time with your friends. Are you intentional in setting aside dedicated moments for them? If not, why not? Consider the reasons why quality time is essential for nurturing deeper connections. How can you create a balance between your commitments and the time you invest in your friendships? Challenge yourself to plan meaningful activities and make the most of the moments you spend together with your friends.

2. **Tune in and truly listen.** In our fast-paced and often distracted world, being attentive and actively listening to our friends can be taxing. Truly tuning in involves setting aside distractions and focusing your full attention on the person. When we actively listen, we show genuine interest in what our friends have to say, creating a safe and supportive space for them to express themselves. It means paying attention not only to their words but also to their nonverbal cues, such as body language and tone of voice. Asking thoughtful questions is also a way to dig deeper into their thoughts and feelings, allowing them to fully express themselves. This kind of attentive listening fosters deeper connections, enhances trust, and strengthens the bond between friends.

- **Envision:** Picture settling into your usual spot at the local diner for Sunday brunch with a friend. As the conversation unfolds, you notice them tracing the rim of their water glass with a distant gaze. You recognize this subtle yet distinct action as a signal of deeper thoughts taking shape. Sensing the need to be fully present, you set your phone aside and devote your entire attention to them. As they begin to open up, you listen intently, maintain eye contact, nod in understanding, and respond thoughtfully. The exchange is not merely about the words spoken; it's about grasping the feelings, concerns, or issues they are attempting to express. In this shared moment of connection, you offer the gift of presence, ensuring your friend feels heard, valued, and understood

- **Reflect:** Recall a recent conversation where you practiced active listening with a friend. How did this deepen your understanding of their experiences and emotions? Do you make it a practice to tune in to your friends' nonverbal communications? Consider how being attentive and actively listening strengthens your bonds with friends. How can you better prioritize active listening in your interactions to deepen your connection with others?

3. **Be generous in action.** Being a truly generous friend goes beyond words; it's about taking tangible actions to enrich your friends' lives.

Keep an eye out for opportunities to bring a smile to their face or offer a helping hand. Whether they're facing a tough time or you simply want to show your appreciation, step up. Surprise them with their favorite snack, invite them over to share a meal, gift them something thoughtful, or lend a hand when they least expect it. These acts of kindness show that you genuinely care and are invested in the friendship. Remember, small acts of generosity go a long way in strengthening your bond and making your friendships more meaningful.

- **Envision:** Imagine that your friend is navigating a particularly hectic schedule right now, weighed down by pressing, high-stakes work deadlines. Knowing that they work from home, you decide to brighten their day by showing up one afternoon with a cup of hot tea from their favorite café. On the cup, you write a special note that says, "You've got this! Keep shining." Your friend is touched by the thoughtful gesture, both by the warm tea and your encouraging words. The in-person exchange, though brief, also re-energized them. It's a moment that goes beyond the ordinary, reinforcing the connection between you.

- **Reflect:** Think back to times when you've gone out of your way to do something special for a friend. How did they react? How did it impact your friendship? Reflect on the ripple effect these acts of kindness had on your bond. How did the joy of brightening their day affect you? Contemplate the power of such gestures in nurturing your relationships. Consider ways you might continue weaving these thoughtful actions into the fabric of your friendships, strengthening your bonds and demonstrating your appreciation for them.

4. **Nurture balance.** Be mindful of maintaining reciprocity in your friendships, where there is a balanced and harmonious exchange of support, care, and generosity. Avoid being the friend who always takes but rarely gives. By practicing reciprocity, you ensure that the relationship is built on fairness and mutual benefit. Stay aware of your friends' needs and make an effort to offer support and care when they need it, just as you would expect them to be there for you. Avoid becoming complacent and taking your friendships for granted. Remember, friendships thrive when there is a healthy give-and-take dynamic.

- **Envision:** Let's say you have a close friend who consistently stands by you, offering advice and support whenever you need it. But, being really honest with yourself, you know that you haven't been as attentive or supportive in return. Recently, they spent hours helping you with a critical job interview, providing insightful feedback and moral support. A few days later, when they shared news of a professional award, you inadvertently shifted the discussion to your own career issues, leading to an awkward silence. Feeling the distance growing between you, your instincts tell you this self-focused tendency might be the cause. Genuinely wanting to repair the bond, you send a heartfelt message: "Lately, I've realized I haven't been as present or as supportive as you've been for me, and I genuinely want to change that. Can we talk about it?" This sincere message paves the way for a meaningful conversation and a renewed and deeper connection in your friendship.

- **Reflect:** Consider a friendship where you have unintentionally taken more than you gave in terms of support and care. How did this shape the dynamics of that relationship? Are your friendships balanced in terms of give and take? As you move forward, what steps can you take to actively engage in reciprocity, ensuring a balanced exchange of attentiveness, care, and support?

5. **Let friends be there for you.** The flip side of reciprocity is allowing your friends to support and give to you. That means embracing the gestures of kindness, help, and support that they offer, understanding that accepting their generosity deepens your friendship bonds. Just like some friends fall into the trap of always receiving without giving, some people also struggle with accepting the generosity of others. It's not uncommon to feel hesitant or uncomfortable when others offer help or support. You may worry about burdening them or have a sense of pride in wanting to be self-reliant. These barriers hinder you from fully embracing the kindness and generosity of your friends. Accepting help or support is not a sign of weakness or dependence; instead, it's a demonstration of trust and vulnerability. By embracing friends' gestures with gratitude and genuine

appreciation, you provide relationships where they feel both valued and important in your life. In essence, allow others the beautiful opportunity to express their love and care for you.

- **Envision:** Imagine you are planning and hosting a milestone birthday party for a parent at your home. You've curated a playlist of their favorite hits and chosen a menu and decorations to recreate the vibe of their youth. You want to be sure every detail is perfect. However, as the day draws near, you start to feel overwhelmed and stressed about managing everything. Noticing your distress, your friend offers to help with decorating the venue and running the last-minute errands. At first, you're hesitant to give up control, feeling that the responsibility lies squarely on your shoulders. Then it dawns on you—allowing your friend to contribute not only eases your stress but also provides them with a chance to show their care and support for you and the guest of honor. Relenting, you express your gratitude for their initiative. With your friend's thoughtful assistance, the celebration comes together seamlessly, and you're able to immerse yourself in the joyous atmosphere, watching the delighted reaction of your parent as they walk into a room full of love, carefully orchestrated with the help of a dear friend.

- **Reflect:** Remember a time you were hesitant to let a friend help you. Why did you hold back? Was it a sense of self-reliance or perhaps the fear of imposing? Think about the outcome when you eventually embraced an offer of help. Reflect on how accepting help can deepen your friendship and build stronger mutual support. How do such experiences reinforce a mutual sense of trust and deepen the connections within your friendships?

6. **Express your gratitude.** Verbalizing gratitude and appreciation to your friends is a powerful way to strengthen and deepen your bonds. Take the time to regularly communicate your thankfulness and acknowledge the impact your friends have on your well-being and happiness. Whether it's stating a simple "thank you" for a kind gesture, giving a compliment to show admiration for their qualities, or a heartfelt text message or a card expressing your deep appreciation, make sure your expressions are sincere and genuine. Let your friends truly feel the warmth in your words. By openly communicating your gratitude, you create a culture where friends are more likely to reciprocate and express their own gratitude in return, serving mutual support and validation.

- **Envision:** You choose a quiet afternoon to sit down and handwrite a thoughtful message on a beautiful card to a friend— it's not their birthday or any special occasion; it's just a spontaneous gesture of appreciation. In the card, you express your deep gratitude for their constant support, love, and friendship. You specifically mention moments when they went above and beyond to be there for you—like the late-night calls they took when you needed advice and the days they spent helping you move to a new apartment. You describe how their presence is so important to your life. You seal the card, add an extra touch with some thoughtful decorations, and send it to your friend. When they receive the card, they call to let you know they were deeply moved by your heartfelt words and the effort you put into expressing your gratitude. They tell you the card has found a special place on their office desk, a constant reminder of the deep connection you both value.

- **Reflect:** How often do you spontaneously express gratitude to your friends? What do you feel when you express appreciation in unexpected and meaningful ways? Do you remember when you last expressed your gratitude to a friend through a handwritten card or letter? How did this personal gesture deepen your connection with them? When you are on the receiving end of such gestures, what is your response? Consider the impact of small, tangible expressions of gratitude and how they can strengthen and nurture your friendships.

7. **Show up through it all.** Being present for your friends during both triumphs and trials is a critical aspect of nurturing and supporting friendships. It means consciously choosing to celebrate their successes and joys, as well as offering a shoulder and an empathetic ear during tougher times. While it's often easy and enjoyable to be there for the good times, the true test of friendship is showing up during the challenging moments. This commitment involves providing

unwavering support and understanding, even when it means confronting or stirring your own discomforts or fears. Consistently standing by your friends through every season of life not only demonstrates your dedication but also solidifies the bond you share and the strength of the friendship.

- **Envision:** Consider a situation where a friend shares with you that their parent has been diagnosed with a serious illness. In this difficult time, you show up for your friend by being a source of comfort, understanding, and support. You offer a listening ear when they call, providing a safe space for them to express their fears and emotions. You also check in with regular texts, and make time for in-person visits to offer the reprieve of laughter or provide a shoulder to lean on when they simply need to be still in their emotions. During an especially challenging week for them, you accompany your friend and their parent to a medical appointment and help with a few household tasks. The active support you give during this hard time shows your friend that they are not alone; they are comforted by the reassurance and stability of your friendship.

- **Reflect:** Pause to think about the last time you showed up for a friend during a difficult situation or a celebratory milestone. How did your presence and support make a difference in their experience? How did it deepen your friendship? Think about times when you didn't show up for the hard times and how you felt after the

> fact? Consider how you can continue to be there for your friends in both joyful and difficult times and how this commitment contributes to the growth and resilience of your relationships.

Friendships flourish when we find harmony in the exchange of giving and receiving. These actions serve as a gentle reminder not to become complacent or lazy in our relationships but to consistently invest effort in their maintenance and nurturing. By staying attentive, practicing reciprocity, and being present during both joyful and challenging moments, we infuse our friendships with positivity and depth. In this chapter, we underlined the significance of expressing gratitude and appreciation to our friends. Through openly acknowledging the positive influence they bring to our lives and genuinely thanking them for their presence and support, we interweave threads of love, appreciation, and mutual care. As you proceed on your journey of nurturing and cultivating your friendships, remember to embrace reciprocity in giving and receiving. Allow this chapter to inspire you to apply these principles and observe how they amplify the positivity in your friendships.

PART III

Growth Tenets

CHAPTER EIGHT

Recalibrating

Most friendships face some amount of conflict, betrayal, or sorrow, with a range of factors determining if and how a friendship ends.[1] *It's crucial to address and resolve these tensions because unresolved strife within friendships—marked by lingering doubts and emotional turmoil—can lead to chronic health issues later on.*[2]

Life is full of changes and transitions, and our friendships are no exception. Sometimes, we find ourselves at a pivotal crossroads where we need to decide whether to recalibrate friendships, making adjustments to better align with the current realities of a friendship, or quit them, ending the relationship when it no longer serves a positive or healthy purpose in our life. A multitude of situational and interpersonal factors play a role in how friendships evolve or dissolve; some of which may be beyond our control.[1 3] But, here's a very important point: Because friendship strain has been linked to impaired physical and emotional health, we can't underestimate the significance of recalibrating our friendships to maintain healthy boundaries, promote personal growth, and enable healing. [2]

Recalibrating may involve a deliberate effort to reestablish equilibrium within a friendship, allowing it to flourish in a balanced way. It might include honest conversations, boundary-setting, or reassessing mutual friendship goals. Sometimes, recalibrating even involves taking a temporary pause to collect your thoughts and emotions or exploring other ways to realign the friendship. It's also important to recognize when it's time to gracefully exit a friendship that no longer serves our well-being and happiness. Quitting a friendship, in this context, doesn't imply a failure but rather a conscious choice to disengage from a friendship that becomes toxic or incompatible with our values and aspirations. While some friendships end abruptly, a majority tend to dissipate slowly, diminishing over time, perhaps making the process more manageable and allowing for the potential of future renewal. This process of recalibration is also particularly poignant in times of loss, such as the death of a friend, when healing may require time, reflection, and the gentle reweaving of our social fabric without their presence. This chapter provides concrete examples and reflective prompts that empower you to navigate these choices effectively, ensuring your friendships align with your overall well-being and happiness.

1. **Embrace changes together**. As we navigate life's changing tides, our personal needs, interests, and priorities naturally evolve. Be open to the idea that your interests, values, and aspirations may evolve, and understand that the same may happen for your friends. Embracing these changes with an open heart and a willingness to communicate can reinforce the bonds of friendship, even as the nature of the relationship transforms. When recalibrating a friendship, engage in open discussions, offering each other the space needed for individual growth. Reach out to trusted individuals, such as close friends or mentors, for support, insights, and perspective during these transitions. This approach ensures that respect and care for one another remain central, even as you both grow and change.

- **Envision:** Consider a close friend you met at your very first job after college, where the shared experience of navigating the new terrain of professional life bonded you in unique ways. This friend has always been career-driven, climbing the ladder with unwavering focus. As the years have passed since college, while they remain intensely career-focused, you are prioritizing your growing family and work-life balance. Your time together is growing less and less frequent. Instead of allowing the friendship to drift due to diverging paths, you initiate a phone conversation. You express your wish to retain the bond, while also understanding your contrasting life phases. You say: "Hey, I know we've been on different paths in recent years. I really treasure our friendship and want to keep it strong, even as our priorities shift. One path isn't better than the other; it's just where we are right now." You continue, "Let's find ways to stay connected that fit into our new realities." They agree, understanding the need for flexibility. Together, you carve out a new routine—perhaps a family-friendly brunch every month, coupled with an occasional late-night chat to catch up on career developments. This conscious recalibration allows your friendship to thrive, respecting each individual's current life stage while preserving the bond you both cherish.

- **Reflect:** Recall a friendship where both of you experienced shifts in needs and priorities. How did you approach recalibrating the dynamics of the relationship? What specific steps did you take to address the changes and preserve a meaningful connection? Consider how this recalibration fostered deeper understanding and bolstered mutual support. Do you have any friendships in your life right now that seem to be changing?

2. **Stay true to your principles.** Authenticity means being true to yourself and acting in ways that align with your genuine thoughts, feelings, and values. It involves being honest and transparent in your interactions with others—without pretending to be someone you're not. Stay true to yourself, and don't force or fake connections with people. While genuine friendships often find their strength in shared beliefs and mutual trust, it's important to recognize when shared values diverge significantly with someone, particularly in new acquaintanceships. If notable differences arise, it's entirely acceptable to prioritize your well-being and consider easing out of relationships that don't resonate with who you are. By doing so, you create space for connections that are more authentic and deeply rewarding.

- **Envision:** You form a friendship with a new colleague, and you connect quite well initially. Over time, you start noticing significant differences in your values and beliefs. These disparities become more apparent in social situations, where their behaviors and principles clash with yours. Instead of forcing the friendship to continue just for the sake of workplace harmony, you trust your instincts. While open communication could be one approach, you opt for a subtler strategy for starters—

gradually reducing interactions, like declining social invites. Your intention is to avoid potential discomfort that might arise from an upfront conversation about ending the friendship. Even so, your coworker persists, sending you messages to meet up for a drink after work. At this juncture, you decide it's time for a more direct approach. With the next invitation, you say: "Lately, I find it works best for me to limit mixing my work and personal life. I appreciate our working relationship and would prefer to keep our interactions more focused in the office environment." The social invitations stopped. While the relationship isn't as chummy as it once was, it feels more authentic.

- **Reflect:** Think about a friendship you stepped back from due to misaligned values. What challenged you most during that time? Did you actively address the differences or allow the friendship to passively drift? Reflect on the choice you made—active or passive—and its implications. How has this experience shaped your approach to forming new friendships? What insights have you gained about when it's best to actively address an issue versus letting things naturally unfold? How does authenticity in relationships factor into these decisions?

3. **Appreciate the seasons of friendship.** Some friendships, just like most things in life, have a lifespan and can naturally fade over time. As we navigate the various stages of life, some friendships

simply don't last. Life events such as relocating, changing jobs, or undergoing significant personal transitions can influence the trajectory of a relationship. It's important to remind yourself that these changes are no one's fault. Rather, they highlight the fact that some friendships, while valuable in the moment, may not be permanent. The friendship was valuable when it needed to be, but perhaps it's not anymore, and that's perfectly okay. The key is to appreciate these friendships for what they are, recognizing their temporality and letting go when necessary without blame.

- **Envision:** Consider a cherished college friend with whom you were inseparable during your academic years. You shared study sessions, laughter, and countless unforgettable memories. Post-graduation, however, the landscape of your lives shifted. Relocating to different cities, embarking on new career paths, and evolving personal priorities led to a gradual decrease in your regular interactions—months turn into years. Sometimes, you feel a twinge of guilt for not maintaining the communication. Yet, when you recall the profound impact and joy that the friendship brought during its prime, you can't help but smile. You recognize that while the dynamics of the friendship evolved, it in no way diminishes the profound significance of the bond you once enjoyed. As a reminder, you affirm to yourself that friendships sometimes have their own season, a unique beauty that leaves an indelible mark on our lives.

- **Reflect:** Think back on a friendship that gradually faded away in your life. How did it affect you during the transition, and how do you perceive the friendship now? Did this experience provide insights into the impermanent nature of certain relationships and the enduring meaning they held during their prime? Reflect on a close friend of the past and allow yourself to recall positive memories.

4. **Weigh the value.** Assessing and reflecting on the quality of friendships is critical to making conscious choices about which relationships to maintain or develop based on their value in your life. Regularly take a few minutes to consider the energy, time, and effort you're putting into each relationship. In a healthy friendship, this investment is reciprocated. The most rewarding relationships are the ones that bring shared joy, mutual support, and a sense of fulfillment. By setting personal standards (and it's okay to have non-negotiables), you shape a clear vision of what constitutes a meaningful and enriching friendship for you and where you want to put your efforts. Remember, friendships are dynamic. They can often weather periods of doubt and come out stronger if both friends are willing to work through the issues.

- **Envision:** You find yourself on a leisurely walk along your community nature trail, the tranquility of your surroundings prompting a moment of reflection. You begin thinking about the various friendships that color your life, considering the energy, time, and affection you invest in each. There's one friendship, in particular, that comes to mind—one that has felt increasingly one-sided for a while. As you pause creek-side for a few minutes, you think about the numerous messages and calls you've initiated, the favors you've happily provided, and the support you've extended during their times of need. Yet, when you look at what you've received in return, you feel unfulfilled. The shared joy and mutual support seem to be waning. You realize that to preserve your well-being and respect your own value, it may be time to reassess this relationship. With clarity and a calm resolve, you decide to have an open conversation with your friend about your feelings, setting the stage for either a reinvigorated connection or a gentle parting of ways. By doing so, you honor not only your own needs but also the integrity of what a fulfilling friendship should be. Your objective isn't about placing blame or withdrawing; it is about understanding and possibly readjusting the dynamic for a healthier and more mutually fulfilling friendship.

- **Reflect:** Consider your current friendships and assess their quality and value in your life. Are there any that stand out for their lack of reciprocity? How do your friendships measure up against your personal standards for a fulfilling relationship? Do they contribute positively to your happiness and sense of belonging, or do they leave you feeling unappreciated and emotionally drained or uncertain? Consider how you might address imbalances. Reflect on whether these friendships warrant a conversation to reestablish mutual effort or if it's time to prioritize your emotional health by letting go.

5. **Handle unhealthy ties.** Friendships should uplift you, yet occasionally they deviate and become unhealthy, draining, or even toxic. Learn to recognize the telltale signs of such detrimental relationships, such as a friendship that consistently raises criticism and negativity, evokes feelings of depression, or encourages unhealthy behaviors. Pay attention to how interactions with certain friends affect your emotional state and energy. If time with a friend usually leaves you feeling depleted or conflicted, consider the necessity of boundaries. Establishing and maintaining these limits is key to protecting your well-being. Addressing these issues with a calm, nonconfrontational approach is best. Use "I" statements to express your feelings and show concern for your friend's well-being, like "I feel hurt when..." or "I'm concerned about you, us because … " If direct conversation is too challenging, stepping back silently can also be a thoughtful choice, allowing time for reflection. If the unhealthy patterns persist despite attempts to address them, it may be necessary to thoughtfully disengage from the friendship. This decision, while challenging, can lead to personal growth and open doors to healthier, more fulfilling connections.

- **Envision:** Let's say you have a neighbor in the apartment next door. Initially, the proximity led to friendly chats in the hallway or an occasional drink shared on your patio. However, over time, these interactions become less pleasant. Every conversation turns into a rant about the other neighbors, their personal woes, or constant criticisms of your lifestyle choices. This starts to drain your energy, and the anticipation of bumping into them is a source of anxiety. To ensure your own peace, you subtly change your approach. You plan ahead for your next encounter and decide on what you will say. Greeting them warmly, you remain concise and authentic in your response by saying, “I feel that our conversations have been leaning toward a lot of negative topics lately. I really need positivity and good vibes in my life, and I hope we can focus on more uplifting discussions.” You don’t want to deepen a friendship with your neighbor, but you also know it’s impossible not to bump into them from time to time. This communicates your genuine feelings while also setting a clear boundary about the kind of interactions you’d like to have.

- **Reflect:** Consider your encounters with unhealthy friendships. What warning signs did you observe, and how did they signal the relationship’s negative impact on you? Reflect on the steps you took to address or end the connection, and the emotions you experienced during this process. With the wisdom you have now, would you approach the situation differently? Consider strategies for managing such friendships in the future, including assertive communication and self-care measures to preserve your well-being. Planning these responses can empower you to act decisively and compassionately should similar circumstances arise again.

6. **Adapt to life's big events.** Recognize how major life events can reshape your friendships. Events like divorce, separation, or relocation—whether experienced by you or your friends—often lead to shifts in friendship dynamics. This might mean you or your friends take sides, or the nature of the relationship changes to accommodate new realities. Though these changes can be uncomfortable—even painful—it's important to remember that such shifts aren't a reflection on the quality of the friendship in its earlier days but rather the evolving circumstances of life.

- **Envision:** Picture yourself going through a tough breakup. Shared couple friends, who initially promised neutrality, are now gravitating more toward your ex-partner. Perhaps it's more convenient for them, or they've known your ex longer. You sense the change—some start canceling plans, others aren't as open in conversations, and a few even completely avoid contact. Instead of jumping to conclusions or harboring resentment, you choose to directly approach three of these friends—all in the same circle—you feel closest to. Over lunch at a neutral café, you say to them, "I've sensed a change in our dynamic since the breakup. I understand this is a difficult situation for everyone involved, and I'd appreciate any clarity or honesty you can provide about our friendship moving forward." By addressing the issue head-on in a positive way, you pave the way for clearer, more genuine interactions, whatever the outcome may be.

- **Reflect:** Think about a time when a significant life event, such as a divorce or a move, affected your friendships. How did you maneuver through these changes? What role did empathy, understanding, and open communication play in managing these shifting dynamics? Would you do anything differently now?

7. **Branch out**. If you choose to dissolve a friendship, recognize that one friendship's evolution can open pathways to new and enriching connections. Adjusting or redefining the dynamics of a friendship isn't necessarily a negative change but rather a necessary step for personal growth, much like pruning a tree to promote its health. As you grow and change, so do your needs and expectations from relationships. By thoughtfully transitioning from certain friendships, you create the emotional room needed for new friendships that resonate more deeply with your current life chapter and aspirations.

- **Envision:** After the difficult decision to part ways with a close friend due to irreconcilable differences, you feel a void in your weekend routines. Seeking to infuse something fresh into your life and make new social connections, you sign up to volunteer at a community initiative that upcycles materials into educational tools for children. At your first gathering in the arts and crafts room of the local elementary school one Saturday morning, while sorting through old magazines and blocks of scrap wood, you strike up a conversation with a fellow volunteer. You both share a passion for education and a belief in sustainable practices. Over time, as you work side by side designing upcycled children's puzzles and flashcards, casual chats evolve into deep discussions about life, shared values, and common goals. This blossoming connection, birthed in the space vacated by an old friendship, not only provides a new volunteer companion but also a confidant who resonates with your current life perspective. This affirms for you that when one chapter ends, another, possibly even more enriching one, begins.

- **Reflect:** Consider an instance where adjusting or concluding a friendship paved the way for fresh connections in your life. How did you embrace these new opportunities? What insights did you gain about the fluid nature of friendships and the importance of embracing change?

8. **Heal and grow when a friend quits you.** Embrace and process the emotions that arise when you are faced with the loss of a friendship, especially when you did not initiate ending the friendship or you lack clarity on the reasons. Use the situation as a catalyst for personal growth. Feelings of hurt, rejection, or confusion are natural responses when a friend chooses to remove themselves from your life. Instead of suppressing these emotions, acknowledge and lean

into them as vital parts of your healing process. Confide your feelings in trusted people who can provide understanding, comfort, and perhaps new insights. Recognize that you might never fully understand the reasons behind their decision, and that's okay. Most likely, the reason has more to do with them than you. The goal isn't to dissect every nuance but to respect their choice while focusing on your own personal growth and healing.

- **Envision:** Your close friend and neighbor, who you've shared countless coffee mornings and late-night chats with, recently decided to pursue a new job opportunity in another city. The bittersweet goodbye was expected, but what you hadn't anticipated was the gradual distancing that crept into your relationship prior to their departure. As they finally move away, your genuine attempts to maintain contact—a text, a call, an email—are consistently met with silence. Instead of allowing yourself to be consumed by feelings of sadness and confusion, you choose a different path. You acknowledge and confront these emotions, seeking solace and understanding from your other close friends, finding comfort in shared experiences and gaining insights from their perspectives. While the exact reason behind your neighbor's emotional withdrawal remains unclear, you accept their decision. You redirect your energy toward nurturing new relationships within your neighborhood, embracing the opportunity for fresh connections and personal growth.

- **Reflect:** Think about a time when a friendship in your life came to an end for unknown reasons. How did you cope with the emotions of hurt and loss? Who stood by you during this challenging period, and in what ways did they provide support? What steps did you take toward focusing on personal growth and healing? Would you handle it differently if faced with a similar situation now?

9. **Mourn illness and death.** The loss of a friend, whether through death or due to debilitating conditions like Alzheimer's disease or a traumatic brain injury, can be a heart-wrenching experience. When a friend passes away, the depth of grief can be overwhelming, yet it's often not as widely acknowledged by society as the loss of a family member. Similarly, witnessing a friend's cognitive decline to the point where they no longer recognize you is its own unique kind of mourning. This pain is often amplified when, despite their physical presence, conditions rob them of the memories of your cherished bond. While society offers rituals and norms for mourning family members, the pain of losing a close friend sometimes feels uncharted. During such challenging times, honor your feelings and permit yourself to grieve fully, whether it's sadness, anger, confusion, or guilt. Lean on loved ones for support, and consider joining support groups or seeking professional help. The journey of grieving a friend is intricate and personal—and real—approach it with compassion and patience.

- **Envision:** Imagine that after years of regular morning walks to the local park and deep conversations on the park benches, your cherished friend, mentor, and neighbor passes away unexpectedly. Now, every morning, as you lace up your walking shoes, their absence hits hard. The park seems too quiet; every bench you pass becomes a reminder of lively debates and shared laughter. Instead of retreating from this pain, you decide to honor the bond you shared by turning a corner of your backyard into a living memorial, planting clusters of their favorite lavender and rosemary. You envision this spot not just as a place of remembrance but as a space of continued conversation and connection. One evening, as the plants begin to thrive, you gather with mutual friends around the garden tribute to share stories and reminisce about the good times spent with your departed friend. This act not only allows you to express your grief but also offers a collective celebration of the beautiful moments shared and promotes healing for everyone involved.

- **Reflect:** Have you ever mourned the death or decline of a friend? How did you manage your grief in a society that does not fully acknowledge the depth of such a loss? Did openly communicating your feelings to others help you during this period? How did you cope and find unique ways to honor their memory? Consider ways that you might balance mourning a friend's absence with celebrating their life.

In this chapter, we explored the often overlooked or unaddressed facet of friendship dynamics: Recalibrating. From establishing boundaries and adjusting friendships to coping with the deep grief of losing a friend, we addressed the full range of emotions these changes bring. It is important to be mindful of these changes and align decisions with your well-being. This includes understanding that not all friendships are meant to last forever. Remember, every friendship is as distinct as the individuals involved. Such uniqueness means there's no one-size-fits-all solution when it comes to adjusting or ending friendships. Your inner voice, enriched by your experiences and feelings, should be your guiding light in these situations. You know better than anyone what feels right for your well-being—trust yourself. While the process of recalibrating or even ending certain friendships isn't easy, there is also an opportunity for introspection, growth, and healing. As you continue on your journey, prioritize your well-being, cherish the memories, embrace the lessons, and always stay true to your values.

CHAPTER NINE

Self-friending

Self-friending is an act of self-compassion, a nonjudgmental understanding of yourself, free from comparisons and evaluations. It's a powerful skill, not just an inherent trait, that you can cultivate to address feelings of inadequacy.[1] *Self-compassion holds the potential to create a happier and more compassionate world for everyone.*[2]

In this chapter, we plunge into the vital importance of friending yourself—the idea of treating yourself with the same kindness, support, and care that you would offer to a friend.

It involves cultivating a positive and nurturing relationship with yourself, acknowledging personal needs, setting healthy boundaries, and practicing self-care and self-compassion. Self-friending means being your own ally and supporter, celebrating your successes, and offering yourself grace during challenging times. These practices don't just stand on their own, though. Befriending yourself creates a path toward genuine and meaningful relationships with others. After all, how we treat ourselves often sets the stage for our friendships.[3] In fact, the way we interact with ourselves often mirrors how we engage with others, setting the tone for the friendships we cultivate. As importantly, embracing a gentle, accepting, and mindful approach toward ourself brings measurable health benefits, reducing stress, anxiety, and depression, while boosting overall well-being.[4]

Here, we'll navigate through seven powerful actions that pave the way for a rich and nourishing relationship with yourself. Let's explore your full potential for becoming your own best friend.

1. **Unmask your authentic self.** Remove any façade or image that you are presenting to the world that isn't a true reflection of your inner self. Dive deep into understanding your individuality and be true to your own personality, spirit, and character. Every quirk, strength, past mistake, and triumph makes you who you are. By acknowledging that you, like everyone else, have strengths and weaknesses, you grow a mindset of self-worth. It's not just about being good enough for friendship; it's about understanding that you're intrinsically worthy. Ensure that you extend to yourself the same kindness and respect that you desire from friends.

- **Envision:** Let's say you've always been a bit of a day-dreamer, something people tease you about from time to time. Rather than dismissing this as a weakness, you embrace it as part of your creativity, a strength that sets you apart. Not only do you stop hiding your day-dreamer self, you claim it openly! Owning this part of yourself boosts your self-confidence and makes you a magnet for genuine connections. Friends are drawn to your unique perspective and imaginative spirit. Your ability to dream, imagine, and think differently becomes a conduit for deeper conversations and shared dreams with friends.

- **Reflect:** Consider the traits and quirks that define you. How do you view your unique traits, and how do these views shape your interactions with friends? Recall a moment when truly embracing yourself influenced a friendship. How can fostering a deeper self-acceptance enrich the bonds you share with others?

2. **Recharge your batteries.** In today's fast-paced world, it's easy to get caught in the whirlwind of busyness. However, constantly running on empty serves no one, especially not yourself. This constant depletion not only affects our personal well-being but also weakens the quality and depth of our friendships. Remember, an exhausted friend can't offer the same level of presence, empathy, or joy as one who's well-rested. Recognize that self-care isn't an indulgence; it's a fundamental necessity. Visualize it as refueling your physical, emotional, and mental tanks. Engage in activities that rekindle your spirit, provide relaxation, and amplify your joy. Whether it's reading a book, practicing meditation, or simply indulging in a quiet afternoon nap, find what revives you. Moreover, it's crucial to set boundaries that protect your energy and time. Contrary to societal beliefs, your worth isn't tied to how packed your schedule is. True reward emerges from how harmoniously you balance activity with rest. So, always remember: Prioritizing your rejuvenation isn't a sign of self-centeredness; it's a testament to understanding the paramount importance of your own well-being.

- **Envision:** Imagine you find solace in gardening. There's something about the feel of the soil between your fingers, the fragrance of flowers, and the satisfaction of watching seeds grow into thriving plants that calms your mind and rejuvenates your spirit. Recognizing this, you consciously carve out time in your hectic schedule to be with your garden daily. This isn't just about maintaining plants; it's a therapeutic ritual. As you prune, water, and nurture each plant, you are simultaneously nurturing your inner self. This immersion in nature doesn't just help you relax; it also equips you with patience, mindfulness, and a renewed vigor—qualities that positively ripple into your friendships. When you're grounded and refreshed, you become a better listener, a more empathetic confidant, and a friend who radiates positivity.

- **Reflect:** Review the rituals or activities that anchor you, providing a sanctuary amid chaos. What does self-care look like in your daily routine? How do these moments of self-care nourish your soul? In what ways does this dedicated time to refuel improve the quality and depth of your interactions with friends?

3. **Journey inward.** Self-reflection isn't just about sitting down with your thoughts for a few minutes. It's about getting to know yourself on a deeper level. It's easy to feel that taking time out for introspection is pulling you away from "more important" tasks, but let's put that myth to rest. This isn't about neglecting other duties; it's about making sure you understand your own needs, values, and aspirations. Gaining clarity about yourself can be achieved through different practices—whether it's reflecting

through journaling, finding presence in mindfulness, seeking solace in prayer with a higher power, or unpacking thoughts with a therapist. The key is choosing a practice that feels true to yourself for genuine self-connection.

- **Envision:** Picture dedicating a quiet time each morning just for yourself: A serene moment with a cup of tea and your journal—a treasured ritual you look forward to. This practice of journaling has evolved into a personal and creative sanctuary, a place where you explore and reflect on your strengths, values, passions, dreams, and even your fears. As your thoughts flow onto the pages, you begin to notice recurring patterns and gain insights into why certain experiences resonate deeply within you. This journey of self-discovery isn't solely about personal growth; it's about cultivating a more authentic, self-awareness that you bring to your friendships. By understanding yourself better, you open the door to understanding others more profoundly as well.

- **Reflect:** Think about a time when self-reflection brought clarity to your life. Consider how you applied this newfound understanding to your relationships. Have you ever felt guilty for taking these moments for personal growth, even if they were beneficial? Ponder why it's essential to dismiss such guilt, recognizing self-reflection as an act of self-care that ultimately enriches your friendships. Lastly, ask yourself if this inner clarity has changed the type of friends you seek or the kind of friend you strive to be.

4. **Show self-compassion.** An essential aspect of befriending yourself is showing compassion toward your own feelings and experiences. Self-compassion is about giving yourself permission to be human, to accept your emotions, and to treat yourself with the same kindness you would offer a friend. In moments of struggle, actively acknowledge and embrace your emotions without self-criticism. Recognize your feelings as the natural ebb and flow of life and respond to your own needs with the same empathy and patience you would extend to a friend. Part of self-compassion is also recognizing when to stand firm and safeguard your well-being. It's okay to not be okay; support yourself with a reassuring inner voice and use that same voice to take a stand outwardly for yourself when necessary. This nurturing practice not only lets you accept your vulnerabilities but also builds resilience and self-advocacy during challenging times.

- **Envision:** See yourself having one of those days when everything feels to be too much—you're swamped at work, your homelife needs attention, and you're grappling with personal challenges. Instead of pushing these feelings aside, you take a moment to genuinely acknowledge your emotional state, reminding yourself that everyone has off days. You gently tell yourself, "It's okay. I've navigated tough times before, and this too shall pass. Just breathe and tackle things one at a time." This self-compassion not only offers you an internal refuge but also strengthens your sense of well-being, allowing you to better connect with friends when you need them most and enhancing your ability to empathize with friends during their own challenges.

- **Reflect:** Recall a time when you felt overwhelmed by life. How did you react to those feelings? Consider whether self-compassion was a part of your response, and if not, how it might have changed the situation. Ponder on acts of self-compassion that you could adopt in future scenarios. Understanding and applying a compassionate awareness can significantly affect how you cope with life's challenges and engage with friends, enhancing mutual support and empathy.

5. **Grow forward.** Invest in your own evolution. Personal growth isn't solely about achieving ambitious career goals or picking up new skills. It's deeper. In other words, personal growth is the continuous journey of transformation, where you expand your mindset, enrich your knowledge, and refine your perspective on life by venturing beyond your comfort zone to embrace the lessons found in new challenges. As you grow and evolve, the depth and authenticity you bring to your friendships also shift. Everyone's growth path is different. But as you move forward, striving to become the most genuine version of yourself, you inadvertently enrich the relationships around you, creating bonds that are rooted in mutual respect and admiration. Who knows—maybe as your friends bear witness to your growth journey, they will become inspired and learn alongside you.

- **Envision:** Imagine you've always been captivated by the vibrant rhythms and rich history of Spain. One day, you decide to dive deeper and enroll in a six-week intensive Spanish language course offered by your local community college. Although you feel intimidated at first, as you immerse yourself, you're not only mastering the language basics, you're also introduced to the world of homemade tapas, tales of flamenco dancers, and stories of historic plazas. Your friends soon take note of your newfound passion. Some, feeling inspired, later join the Spanish class, while others eagerly anticipate the Spanish-themed dinners you now host. Your dive into linguistic and cultural discovery not only broadens your own horizons but also serves as a connecting thread, drawing you and your friends into a rich tapestry of shared experiences and stories, deepening your bonds.

- **Reflect:** Remember a time when you consciously worked on your personal growth. It could be an interest you pursued, a cause you championed, or a lifestyle change. How did this experience of growth shape your self-perception? How did your friends react to this change? Did this personal growth enrich your interactions and relationships with your friends?

6. **Savor pleasure and enjoyment.** Make sure to regularly do things that make you happy and satisfied, releasing those wonderful

neurotransmitters like dopamine. It could be anything from immersing yourself in a good book, taking long walks on a sunny day, going dancing, cooking a new recipe, or simply treating yourself to a leisurely afternoon completely unscheduled. Whatever the activity, the key is that it's something you truly enjoy, not something you think you should enjoy or something that others expect you to enjoy. By indulging in these personal joys, you cultivate a vibrant inner life. And a happier you invariably leads to a more lively and positive presence in your friendships.

- **Envision:** Let's say you have a deep enjoyment of yoga, yet the demands of everyday life caused it to gradually fade into the background. Feeling a sense of restlessness within your daily routine, you make a conscious choice to reignite this passion. You set up a designated space in your home, find an online program that speaks to you, and every Sunday morning you carve out thirty minutes for this rejuvenating and calming practice. By doing so, you are not only rekindling your passion but also nurturing a positive and joyful relationship with yourself. The nourishment you provide to your own well-being translates into an extra spring in your step, allowing you to approach your friendships with a greater sense of fulfillment, contentment, and engagement.

- **Reflect:** Consider activities that genuinely light you up. How often do you make time for them? What barriers do you face in pursuing them, and how can you overcome these obstacles? How does prioritizing self-enjoyment impact your overall well-being and the energy you bring into your friendships?

7. **Affirm and celebrate self-worth.** Cultivate a practice of speaking positively to and about yourself. Embrace empowering language that recognizes your inherent worth and capabilities. Remind yourself that you are worthy of friendship, and people want to be friends with you because you bring unique qualities to the table. Positive self-talk isn't just self-help jargon—it's actually backed by solid research.[5] [6] Think of it as having a personal motivator that's always available. When you practice talking to yourself in a positive and encouraging way, you're doing more than just boosting your mood and confidence. You're building up resilience, enhancing your self-esteem, and even rewiring your brain to stay motivated. It's a simple yet powerful tool that's right at your fingertips, and it has the potential not only to truly improve your mental, emotional, and physical well-being but also has a ripple effect on your friendships, enhancing the positivity you bring to them.

- **Envision:** Imagine starting each morning by grounding yourself with affirmations in front of the mirror. As you look into your own eyes, you repeat statements like "I am surrounded by love from my friends," "I am worthy of meaningful and fulfilling friendships," and "I bring love and positive energy to my friendships." These affirmations hold profound power beyond mere words; they shape your mindset. When challenges arise, they transform into opportunities for you to demonstrate resilience and inner strength. Incorporating these affirmations daily isn't just about boosting your self-worth; it transforms the way you engage with your friendships. You interact with confidence, authenticity, and gratitude, deepening the bonds and enriching the shared experience.

- **Reflect:** Think about your self-talk. When was the last time you looked in a mirror and said something kind to yourself? What positive affirmations resonate with you personally? Name a few right now. How and when can you seamlessly integrate these affirmations into your daily routine? In what ways does positive self-talk improve how you perceive yourself and interact with friends?

As we bring this chapter on how to befriend ourselves to a close, take some time to truly appreciate the significance of becoming your own best friend. Every step you take toward embracing your uniqueness, every effort you put into taking care of your physical, mental, and emotional well-being, and every moment you spend reflecting on your thoughts, feelings, and experiences contribute to this enriching journey. Show yourself the compassion you'd extend to a dear friend, invest in your personal growth, and savor activities that bring you joy and fulfillment.

Remember, these aren't just hollow actions—they're stepping stones to nurturing a profound relationship with yourself; actions that also set the stage for meaningful friendships to flourish. This journey of self-discovery and self-love paves the way for not only deep connections with others but also a healthier, more satisfying and fulfilling life. Embrace your journey with open arms and a willing heart, and watch as it not only enriches your relationship with yourself but also elevates your friendships. Be your own best friend, and let the magic of true friendship unfold in your life.

CHAPTER TEN

Closing Reflections

As we conclude Friends Matter, for Life, *spend some time reflecting on the new insights that deepened your understanding of these invaluable relationships. Throughout the pages of this book, we probed the complexities of adult friendships, gaining a deep appreciation for their ties to our own happiness and the challenges they sometimes present. But remember, your journey of friendship does not end here. Friendships, like each of us, are living, breathing entities, always in flux, and they flourish with ongoing attention and care. Let this book serve as a guiding light as you continue to navigate these dynamic bonds.*

Here's a quick recap of the eight tenets of the Framework of Dynamic Friendship imparted throughout this journey:

1. **Recognizing:** First and foremost, we've grasped the importance of identifying and acknowledging the varied roles our friends fill in our lives. Understanding and cherishing these roles help us cultivate diverse, rewarding friendships that weather the test of time.
2. **Communicating:** Communication, the keystone of any significant bond, shines in the spotlight. Actively

listening, expressing ourselves genuinely, and showing empathy build a solid foundation of trust and authenticity in our friendships.

3. **Accepting:** Never underestimate the power of acceptance. When we embrace our friends' uniqueness, quirks, and imperfections, we develop the grace to navigate life's inevitable rough patches, ultimately nurturing deeper connections.
4. **Blending:** Find delight in uniting various friends, romantic partners, and family members. This merging of different social circles leads to shared experiences and creates a vibrant, intricate mosaic of friendship.
5. **Safeguarding:** Trust and loyalty stand firm as the pillars of our friendships. Standing by our friends, providing unwavering support, and defending them during challenges form bonds resilient enough to withstand life's storms.
6. **Reciprocating:** Friendships are a dance of giving and receiving. Balancing selflessness with open acceptance of support fosters a reciprocal exchange of kindness, nurturing growth and positivity for all involved.
7. **Recalibrating:** At times, friendships may demand recalibration. Discerning when to adjust, amicably part ways, or even grieve is crucial for our personal growth and mental health. Change is, after all, constant.
8. **Self-friending:** Finally, remember the most vital of friendships is the one we keep with ourselves. By prioritizing self-care, practicing self-reflection, and nurturing self-acceptance, we position ourselves to be the best friend we can be. After all, a nurtured self shines brightly in any friendship.

It's an undeniable fact: Friends truly matter—for life. They're not just company. They're our lifelines, our joy-bringers, and pivotal to our overall well-being. In a world where loneliness often casts its long shadow, friendships are beacons of light, offering solace, connection, and a sense of belonging. They have the potential to stand as a powerful solution to the loneliness and solitude that sometimes creep into our lives.

Yet, cultivating genuine friendships is not a one-way street. It demands our commitment to being as good a friend as we hope to find, our willingness to invest time in these connections, and our capacity to adapt and evolve together. Yes, like any meaningful relationship, friendships do require effort and intention. But the rewards—laughter shared, burdens eased, and memories made—are immeasurable and make every moment of investment worthwhile.

Friendship is undoubtedly a vital aspect of our lives, yet as adults, we often find ourselves navigating its intricacies without a clear road map. The journey of maintaining long-standing friendships while also forging new connections is both rewarding and challenging. We're faced with the task of balancing the nostalgia and familiarity of old friends with the excitement and uncertainty of new ones. In a world where time and responsibilities often pull us in various directions, the art of nurturing existing bonds and cultivating fresh ones requires careful consideration and a willingness to adapt. But, within these pages, we uncovered the power to shape a new narrative—a power that resides within each of us, fueled by newfound knowledge, introspection, and decisive action. This book reaches into the heart of these complexities, providing insights, strategies, and reflections to help us navigate the dynamic terrain of adult friendships with authenticity, grace, and intention.

Dynamic friendships are organic, marked by their capacity for growth, resilience in the face of change, and the flexibility to adapt. At the core of dynamic friendships is open communication, unwavering mutual support, and a heartfelt exchange of love, kindness, and respect that transforms us, making us better together than we ever were apart. In these relationships, we are called to action—to consistently nurture, to grow alongside each other, and to meet life's ups and downs together. These friendships are not static; instead, they evolve over time, allowing room for personal growth, shared histories, and enduring bonds. It's through time together, filled with both laughter and tears, that our friendships find their true form, enriching our lives with their depth and warmth. So, remember to hold your friendships in the highest regard. As we navigate the unpredictable seas of life, it is the strength found in friendship that steadies us against the tides. In the end, the bonds of friendship truly matter—for life!

Notes

Chapter One

1. Dunbar, R. M. "The Anatomy of Friendship." *Trends Cogn Sci* 22, no. 1 (2018): 32-51. doi: 10.1016/j.tics.2017.10.
2. Hung, L.W., et al. "Gating of Social Reward by Oxytocin in the Ventral Tegmental Area." *Science* 357 (2017): 1406-1411. doi: 10.1126/science.aan4994.
3. Romero, T., Onishi, K., and Hasegawa, T. "The Role of Oxytocin on Peaceful Associations and Sociality in Mammals." *Behaviour* 153, no. 9-11 (2016): 1053-1071. doi:10.1163/1568539X-00003358.
4. van der Horst, M., and Coffé, H. "How Friendship Network Characteristics Influence Subjective Well-Being." *Soc Indic Res* 107, no. 3 (2012): 509-529. doi: 10.1007/s11205-011-9861-2.
5. Waldinger, R. *The Good Life: Lessons from the World's Longest Scientific Study of Happiness*. Simon and Schuster, 2023.
6. Lu, P., Oh, J., Leahy, K. E., and Chopik, W. J. "Friendship Importance Around the World: Links to Cultural Factors, Health, and Well-Being." *Front. Psychol.* 11 (2021): 570839. doi: 10.3389/fpsyg.2020.570839.
7. Muraco, A. *Couples: Friendships at the Intersection of Gender and Sexual Orientation*. Duke University Press, 2012.

8. Buecker, S., Mund, M., Chwastek, S., Sostmann, M., and Luhmann, M. "Is Loneliness in Emerging Adults Increasing over Time? A Preregistered Cross-Temporal Meta-Analysis and Systematic Review." *Psychol Bull* 147, no. 8 (2021): 787-805. doi: 10.1037/bul0000332.
9. Hawkley, L.C., and Cacioppo, J.T. "Loneliness Matters: A Theoretical and Empirical Review of Consequences and Mechanisms." *Ann Behav Med.* 40, no. 2 (2010): 218-27. doi:10.1007/s12160-010-9210-8.
10. Thygesen, H., Lamph, G., Kabelenga, I., and Geirdal, A. "Associations Between Social Media Use and Loneliness in a Cross-National Population: Do Motives for Social Media Use Matter?" *Health Psychol Behav Med.* 11, no. 1 (2023). doi: 10.1080/21642850.2022.2158089.
11. Vieth, G., Rothman, A. J., and Simpson, J. A. "Friendship Loss and Dissolution in Adulthood: A Conceptual Model." *Curr Opin Psychol* 43 (2022): 171-175. doi: 10.1016/j.copsyc.2021.07.007.
12. Bhattacharya, K., Ghosh, A., Monsivais, D., Dunbar, R. I., and Kaski, K. "Sex Differences in Social Focus Across the Life Cycle in Humans." *R Soc Open Sci* 3, no. 4 (2016). doi: 10.1098/rsos.160097.
13. Ng, Y. T., Huo, M., Gleason, M. E., Neff, L. A., Charles, S. T., and Fingerman, K. L. "Friendships in Old Age: Daily Encounters and Emotional Well-Being." *J Gerontol B Psychol Sci Soc Sci* 76, no. 3 (2021): 551-562. doi: 10.1093/geronb/gbaa007.
14. "American Time Use Survey," United States Bureau of Labor Statistics, 2022.
15. Goddard, Isabel. "What Does Friendship Look Like in America?" Pew Research Center. October 12, 2023. https://www.pewresearch.org/short-reads/2023/10/12/what-does-friendship-look-like-in-america/.
16. Fuller-Iglesias, H. R., Webster, N. J., and Antonucci, T. C. "Adult Family Relationships in the Context of Friendship." *Research in Human Development* 10, no. 2 (2013): 184-203. doi: 10.1080/15427609.2013.786562.
17. Dunbar, Robin M. *Friends: Understanding the Power of Our Most Important Relationships.* Little, Brown and Company: 2021.
18. Webster, adapted.
19. Cohen, Y. A. "Patterns of Friendship." *Social Structure and Personality,* edited by Cohen Y. A., 351–386. New York: Holt, Rinehart and Winston, 1966.
20. Baumgarte, R. "Conceptualizing Cultural Variations in Close Friendships." *Online Readings in Psychology and Culture* 5, no. 4 (2016). doi: 10.9707/2307-0919.1137.
21. Demir, M., Özen, A., and Procsal, A. D. "Friendship and Happiness." *Encyclopedia of Quality of Life and Well-Being Research.* Springer, Dordrecht: 2014. doi: 10.1007/978-94-007-0753-53895.

Chapter Two

1. Ho, C. Y. "Better Health With More Friends: The Role of Social Capital in Producing Health." *Health Econ.* 25 (2015): 91–100. doi: 10.1002/hec.3131.
2. Holt-Lunstad, J., Smith, T. B., and Layton, J. B. "Social Relationships and Mortality Risk: A Meta-Analytic Review." *PLoS Medicine* 7, no. 7 (2010).
3. Lu, P., Oh, J., Leahy, K. E., and Chopik, W. J. "Friendship Importance Around the World: Links to Cultural Factors, Health, and Well-Being." *Front. Psychol.* 11 (2021): 570839. doi: 10.3389/fpsyg.2020.570839.
4. Anderson, A. R., and Fowers, B. J. "An Exploratory Study of Friendship Characteristics and Their Relations with Hedonic and Eudaimonic Well-Being." *J. Soc. Pers. Relat.* 37 (2020): 260–280. doi: 10.1177/0265407519861152.

Chapter Three

1. Hammer, B. "Why Good Communication is the Foundation of Enduring True Friendship." *Deepening Your Personal Relationships: Developing Emotional Intimacy and Good Communication.* Strategic Book Publishers, 2014.
2. Altman, I., and Taylor, D. A. *Social Penetration: The Development of Interpersonal Relationships.* Holt, Rinehart and Winston, 1973.
3. Berger, C. R., and Roloff, M. E. *Handbook of Interpersonal Communication* (5th ed.). SAGE Publications, 2019.
4. Liloia, N. "Out of Touch: The Benefits of Physical Touch, and What Happens When We Don't Get Enough." *The Synapse: Intercollegiate Science Magazine* 25, no.1 (2020).

Chapter Four

1. Ciarrochi, J., et al. "When Empathy Matters: The Role of Sex and Empathy in Close Friendships." *Journal of Personality* 85 (2016). doi: 10.1111/jopy.12255.
2. Morelli, S. A., Ong, D. C., Makati, R., Jackson, M. O., and Zaki, J. "Empathy and Well-Being Correlate with Centrality in Different Social Networks." *Proc Natl Acad Sci USA* 114, no. 37 (2017): 9843-9847. doi: 10.1073/pnas.1702155114.
3. Meuwese, R., Cillessen, A. H. N., and Güroğlu, B. "Friends in High Places: A Dyadic Perspective on Peer Status as Predictor of Friendship Quality and the Mediating Role of Empathy and Prosocial Behavior." *Social Development* 26, no. 3 (2017): 503–519. doi: 10.1111/sode.12213.

4. Hawkley L.C., Hughes M.E., Waite L.J., Masi C.M., Thisted R.A., and Cacioppo J.T. "From Social Structural Factors to Perceptions of Relationship Quality and Loneliness: The Chicago Health, Aging, and Social Relations Study." *J Gerontol B Psychol Sci Soc Sci* 63, no. 6 (2008): 375-84. doi: 10.1093/geronb/63.6.s375.

Chapter Five

1. Cohen, S., and Janicki-Deverts, D. "Can We Improve Our Physical Health by Altering Our Social Networks?" *Perspect Psychol Sci* 4, no. 4 (2009): 375-378. doi: 10.1111/j.1745-6924.2009.01141.x.
2. Fingerman, K. L., Huo, M., Charles, S. T., and Umberson, D. J. "Variety Is the Spice of Late Life: Social Integration and Daily Activity." *The Journals of Gerontology: Series B: Psychological Sciences and Social Sciences* 75 (2020): 377–388. doi: 10.1093/geronb/gbz007.
3. Kang, W. "Understanding the Associations Between the Number of Close Friends and Life Satisfaction: Considering Age Differences." *Front. Psychol.* 14 (2023). doi: 10.3389/fpsyg.2023.1105771.

Chapter Six

1. Rempel, J. K., Ross, M., and Holmes, J. G. "Trust and Communicated Attributions in Close Relationships." *Journal of Personality and Social Psychology* 81, no. 1 (2001): 57-64. doi: 10.1037/0022-3514.81.1.57.
2. Rotter, J. "A New Scale for the Measurement of Interpersonal Trust." *Journal of Personality* 35 (1967): 651-665. doi: 10.1111/j.1467-6494.1967.tb01454.x.
3. Yavuz Güler, Ç., Çakmak, I., and Bayraktar, E. "Never Walk Alone on the Way: Friendships of Emerging Adults." *Personal Relationships* 29, no. 4 (2022): 811–839. doi: 10.1111/pere.12455.

Chapter Seven

1. Lemay, E. P., and Clark, M. S. "'Walking on Eggshells'": How Expressing Relationship Insecurities Perpetuates Them." *Journal of Personality and Social Psychology* 95, no. 2 (2008): 420-441. doi: 10.1037/0022-3514.95.2.420.
2. Banerjee, P. *The Power of Positivity: Optimism and the Seventh Sense.* SAGE Publishing India, 2018.
3. Pezirkianidis, C., Galanaki, E., Raftopoulou, G., Moraitou, D., and Stalikas, A. "Adult Friendship and Well-Being: A Systematic Review with Practical Implications." *Front Psychol* 14 (2023). doi: 10.3389/fpsyg.2023.1059057.

Chapter Eight

1. Vieth, G., Englund, M. M., and Simpson, J. A. "Developmental Antecedents of Friendship Satisfaction in Adulthood." *Developmental Psychology* 58, no. 12 (2022): 2401-2412. doi: 10.1037/dev0001437.
2. Chopik, W. J. "Associations Among Relational Values, Support, Health, and Well-Being Across the Adult Lifespan." *Personal Relationships* 24, no. 2 (2017): 408-422. doi: 10.1111/pere.12187.
3. Franco, M. G. *Platonic: How the Science of Attachment Can Help You Make—and Keep—Friends*. Penguin, 2022.

Chapter Nine

1. Neff, K. D. "Self-Compassion, Self-Esteem, and Well-Being." *Social and Personality Psychology Compass* 5, no. 1 (2011): 1–12. doi: 10.1111/j.1751-9004.2010.00330.x.
2. Neff, K. D. "Self-Compassion: Theory, Method, Research, and Intervention." *Annu Rev Psychol* 74 (2023): 193-218. doi: 10.1146/annurev-psych-032420-031047.
3. Germer, C. *The Mindful Path to Self-Compassion: Freeing Yourself from Destructive Thoughts and Emotions*. The Guilford Press, 2009.
4. Homan, K. J., and Sirois, F. M. "Self-Compassion and Physical Health: Exploring the Roles of Perceived Stress and Health-Promoting Behaviors." *Health Psychology Open* 4, no. 2 (2017). doi: 10.1177/2055102917729542.
5. Franco, M. G. *Platonic: How the Science of Attachment Can Help You Make—and Keep—Friends*. Penguin, 2022.
6. Brown, Brené. *The Gifts of Imperfection: Hazelden Information and Educational Services*. 2010.

Acknowledgments

With heartfelt gratitude, I extend my thanks to Amplify Publishing Group for their unwavering belief in both me and my vision for this book from the very beginning; a special mention to Lauren Magnussen for her guidance and for keeping me focused on our end goal. I also want to express my appreciation to Michelle Gerside and the talented group at Soul Camp Creative, as well as Noah Levy, for their unique ability to truly see me and aid in seeing myself in my entirety. This book would not have come to fruition and found its place in the world without each of you.

About the Author

An esteemed professor and research psychologist, Dr. Kimberly Horn has worked with top-tier academic institutions, including West Virginia University, The George Washington University, and Virginia Tech. Devoting her career to helping others lead healthier, happier, and more connected lives, she has conducted nearly three decades of health behavior research with an extensive publication record. Her contributions have garnered recognition and accolades on a global scale. Praised for her engaging and compassionate style, Dr. Horn has shared her work with diverse audiences, from community town hall meetings to large-scale international conferences. Her ability and intention to connect underscore her commitment to helping people understand the reasons behind certain health behaviors and navigate their complex social terrain™ with confidence.

Dr. Horn's background sets the stage for her literary debut, *Friends Matter, for Life*. A natural extension of her work, the book addresses how integral friendships are to our emotional and physical well-being. At a time when the shadow of loneliness looms large in our world, *Friends Matter, for Life* emerges as a beacon of hope. Blending her in-depth understanding of health behavior with her natural love for storytelling, Dr. Horn instills trust as she guides readers toward a deeper intention to cultivate and appreciate friendship's vital role in our adult lives.

Residing in Pittsburgh, Pennsylvania, Dr. Horn cherishes life's simple pleasures alongside her spouse and their delightfully fluffy doodle, a testament to the loving connections she values and writes about.